HURTIGRUTEN®

The world's most beautiful sea voyage

D0104846

Text:
Erling Storrusten

© Published by Hurtigruten by
Ofotens og Vesteraalens Dampskibsselskab AS/Narvik
Troms Fylkes Dampskipsselskap AS/Tromsø

Concept/design/layout: Reiselivsutvikling Reklame AS, Bergen
Charts/Maps: Statens Kartverk
Translated by: COM TEXT AS/NORICOM AS
Lithography: SP-Repro AS, Bergen
Printed by: ERA-Trykk AS, Bergen
Circulation: English 25.000, 7. edition 05-2002
ISBN 82-993154-4-1

INDEX......

Side

History...6
Introduction to the Coastal Express............................... 8

Day 1 Leaving Bergen through the islands 12
Day 2 Måløy - Geiranger - Molde.............................18
Day 3 Trondheim - Rørvik 32
Day 4 The Arctic Circle - Stamsund 40
Day 5 Harstad - Skjervøy 50
Day 6 Havøysund - Mehamn....................................62
Day 7 Vadsø - Kirkenes - Berlevåg 70
Day 8 Havøysund -Skjervøy 80
Day 9 Harstad - Trollfjorden - Lofoten - Stamsund...........88
Day 10 The Arctic Circle - Rørvik 100
Day 11 Trondheim - Kristiansund 108
Day 12 Måløy - Bergen 118

Subjects:
The Gulf Stream 17
Bird colonies...28
Birds to be seen en route 30
The Arctic Circle 39
The Northern Lights - Aurora Borealis 61
Wind power..61
The Sami..69
The Midnight Sun and its cycle................................78
Whaling and seal hunting 98
Aqua culture / Fish farming...................................99
Oil and gas...116
Norwegian territorial waters - economic zone and the Continental Shelf .126

Chart 128
Key to route map...130

In 1891, August Kriegsman Gran, the national steamship advisor, came up with the idea of providing an express boat service between Trondheim and Hammerfest. Two steamship companies, Det Nordenfjeldske Dampskibsselskab and Det Bergenske Dampskibsselskap, were offered the route, but turned it down as sailing during the dark and stormy winters was considered impossible. At the time, only two marine charts existed and there were only 28 lighthouses north of Trondheim.

Vesteraalens Dampskibsselskab, a relatively young steamship company based in Stokmarknes, took up the challenge. For some time, Captain Richard With and his pilots had been keeping accurate notes on courses, speeds and times taken to sail the route and felt that the service would be viable. A compass and a clock were the only navigational aids necessary in the Polar Night.On 18 May 1893, the government entered into a 4-year contract with Vesteraalens Dampskibsselskab, providing the company with the   backing for a weekly sailing between Trondheim and Hammerfest during the summer and Trondheim and Tromsø during the winter. There were nine ports of call on the route.

On the morning of 2 July 1893, the steamship 'Vesteraalen' left Trondheim for Hammerfest. This started a communications revolution, giving industry and coastal inhabitants better access to the outside world. Letters from Trondheim, which had previously taken up to three weeks to reach Hammerfest during the summer, and five months during the winter, could now be delivered by the Coastal Express in just a few days.

«Richard With» was built at Trondheims Mek. Verksted and put into traffic in June 1909. (Photo: Mittet Foto AS, Sjøfartsmuseet, Bergen)

Svolvær was reached in 36 hours - and 67 hours after leaving Trondheim, the ship dropped anchor in Hammerfest harbour on 5 July at 03.30 - half an hour early! The ship and its crew were greeted with salutes and cheering all along the coast.

Once Richard With and Vesteraalens Dampskibsselskab had shown the way, several shipping companies followed. In 1894, Det Bergenske Dampskibsselskab and Det Nordenfjeldske Dampskibsselskab were granted permission to operate ships on the route. The number of ships serving the route constantly increased. In 1898, Bergen became the southernmost port on the Coastal Express' route. Vadsø was included on the route in 1907 and Kirkenes in 1914. For a short period, there were weekly sailings from Stavanger but, from 1936 to the present day a Coastal Express has left Bergen daily heading north. This service was only interrupted by the war.

Over the 100 years of the Coastal Express' operation, more than 70 ships have been used on the route. The first ships were taken from other Norwegian domestic or foreign routes. Eventually, ships were specially constructed for the Coastal Express. These were equipped with refrigerated compartments, roll on/roll off facilities, vehicle holds, as well as course and conference facilities. They were specially designed for loading pallets and were single class ships.

From its conception, it was believed that tourism would form the basis of the Coastal Express' operations. Early on, brochures were printed in several languages promoting the Coastal Express and the wild and beautiful Norwegian coastline. These were distributed to travel agents and individual customers abroad.

The advent of the Coastal Express meant that places such as the Lofoten Islands, Troll Fjord, Skjervøy Island, Hammerfest and the North Cape became accessible to international travellers who wanted to visit the Land of the Midnight Sun. Tourists came in their thousands, making the Coastal Express one of Europe's biggest attractions.

Today, the route is internationally known as 'The world's most beautiful sea voyage'. There's nothing else like it anywhere in the world.

Companies involved with the Coastal Express.

1893	Vesteraalens Dampskibsselskab
1894-1979	Det Bergenske Dampskibsselskab
1895-1989	Det Nordenfjeldske Dampskibsselskab
1919-1979	Det Stavangerske Dampskibsselskab
1936	Ofotens Dampskibsselskab
1945-1958	Det Nordlandske Dampskibsselskab
1979	Troms Fylkes Dampskibsselskab
1987	Ofotens Dampskibsselskab and Vesteraalens Dampskibsselskab merged.
1988-1996	Finnmark Fylkesrederi og Ruteselskap

INTRODUCTION TO THE COSTAL EXPRESS......

M/S «Nordnorge».
Operator: Ofotens og Vesteraalens
Dampskibsselskab AS, Narvik. (Photo: TO-FOTO Ⓜ)

M/S «Nordkapp».
Operator: Ofotens og Vesteraalens Damp-
skibsselskab AS, Narvik. (Photo: H.M. Valderhaug)

M/S «Polarlys».
Operator: Troms Fylkes Dampskibsselskap AS,
Tromsø. (Photo: Ulstein International)

M/S «Nordlys».
Operator: Troms Fylkes Dampskibsselskap AS,
Tromsø. (Photo: TO-FOTO)

M/S «Richard With».
Operator: Ofotens og Vesteraalens
Dampskibsselskab AS, Narvik. (Photo: TO-FOTO)

M/S «Kong Harald».
Operator: Troms Fylkes Dampskibsselskap AS,
Tromsø. (Photo: TO-FOTO)

M/S «Vesterålen».
Operator: Ofotens og Vesteraalens
Dampskibsselskab AS, Narvik. (Photo: Helge Sunde)

M/S «Narvik».
Operator: Ofotens og Vesteraalens
Dampskibsselskab AS, Narvik. (Photo: TO-FOTO)

M/S «Midnatsol».
Operator: Troms Fylkes Dampskibsselskap AS,
Tromsø. (Photo: TO-FOTO)

M/S «Finnmarken».
Operator: Ofotens og Vesteraalens
Dampskibsselskab AS, Narvik.

M/S «Trollfjord».
Operator: Troms Fylkes Damp-
skibsselskap AS, Tromsø.

	M/S «Nordnorge»	M/S «Nordkapp»	M/S «Polarlys»	M/S «Nordlys»	M/S «Richard With»
Operator	OVDS	OVDS	TFDS	TFDS	OVDS
Year of building	1997	1996	1996	1994	1993
Shipyard	Kværner Kleven	Kværner Kleven	Ulstein Verft	Wolkswerft	Wolkswerft
Location	Ulsteinvik	Ulsteinvik	Ulsteinvik	Stralsund	Stralsund
Country of origin	Norway	Norway	Norway	Germany	Germany
Last refit	-	-	-	-	-
Gross tonnage	11.350	11.386	11.341	11.200	11.200
Overall length	123,3	123,3	123	121,8	121,8
Greatest width	19,5	19,5	19,5	19,2	19,2
Displacement	4,7	4,7	4,7	4,7	4,7
Main engine	2xMAK 6M552C	2xMAK 6M552C	2xBRM9+2xKRG9	2xMAK 6M552C	2xMAK 6M552C
Gross horsepower	12,240	12,240	15,900	12.240	12.240
Bow propeller	2	2	2	2	2
Stern propeller	2	2	2	-	-
Cruise speed in knots	18	18	18	18	18
Passengers	691	691	737	700	700
Bunk capacity	464	490	480	490	490
Vehicle capacity	45	45	50	50	50
Load area in m^2	300	350	1100	950	950

M/S «Kong Harald»	M/S «Vesterålen»	M/S «Narvik»	M/S «Midnatsol»	M/S «Finnmarken»	M/S «Trollfjord»
TFDS	OVDS	OVDS	TFDS	OVDS	TFDS
1993	1983	1982	1982	2002	2002
Wolkswerft	Kaarbøe	Aker Trøndelag	Ulstein Hatlø	Kværner Kleven	Fosen Mek. Verkst.
Stralsund	Harstad	Trondheim	Ulsteinvik	Ulsteinvik	Rissa
Germany	Norway	Norway	Norway	Norway	Norway
-	1995	1995	1988	-	-
11.200	4.072	4.072	6.167	15.000	15.000
121,8	108,55	108,55	108,55	138,5	135,5
19,2	16,52	16,52	16,52	21,5	21,5
4,7	4,6	4,6	4,6	4,95	4,9
2xMAK 6M552C	2xBergen KVM-16	2xBergen KVM-16	2xBergen KVM-16	2xWärtsilä	2xWärtsilä
12.240	6.400	6.400	6.400	18.490	10.728
2	2	2	2	2	2
-	-	-	-	1	2
18	17,5	17,5	17,5	18	18
700	580	580	580	1000	1000
490	314	308	308	643	674
50	40	40	40	47	50
950	1.200	1.200	1.200	359	490

DAY 1. LEAVING BERGEN THROUGH THE ISLANDS.......

N
W   E
S

Brattvåg
Valderøya
Giske   Ålesund lufthavn   Søvik   Vat
Godøy   **Ålesund**   Spjelkavik
Svinøy Fyr   Runde   Langevåg   Sula   Sl
Fosnavåg   *Torvik*   Harbid   Storfjorden   Sykky
Herøy   Ulsteinvik   Hjørungavåg
Vestkapp   Dolsteinshola   Vartdalsfjorden
Stadhavet   Ervik   Gurskøy
Stadlandet   Stanylysfjorden
   Ørsta
Kråkenes Fyr   Skongenes Fyr   **Volda**
Einevarden   Selje
Klovningen   Vågsøy   Kloster
Veststeinen   *Måløy*   Raudeberg
Bremanger   Nordfjord   Nordfjordeid
Hornelen   Strym
Frøya   Vingen   Lo
Kalvåg   Svelgen   Olde
Frøysjøen   Botnane
Hovden   Ålfotbreen
Batalden   **Hjelmeset**
Stabben Fyr   Sandane
Ytterøyane Fyr   Skorpa   **Florø**   Jostedalsbreen
Kinn   Florø Lufthavn
Askrova   Svanøy   Naustdal   Jølster
Stavenes   Førdefjorden
Askvoll   **Førde**
Atløy   Dale
Alden   Korssund   Førde Lufthavn   Fjærland
Vilnesfjorden
Ospa   Hyllestad
Gåsvær   Vadheim   Høyanger
Utvær Fyr   Sula   Balestrand
Solund Kirke   Leirvik   Herman
Steinsundet   Sognefjorden   Leikanger
Ytre Sula
Eivindvik   Viksøyri
Sogneoksen   Gulafjorden
Holmengrå Fyr   Stølsheimen
Fedje   Vardøtangen   Gudvangen
Fensfjorden
Hellisøy Fyr   Mongstad
Hellesøy   Radøy   Myr
Sture   Manger   Dale   Ulvik
Herdla   Stanghelle
Holsnøy   Alver   Vaksdal   Ålvik
Kolfsnes   Knarvik   Eidfjore
Salhus   Øystese
Øygarden   Agotnes   Ytre Arna   Voss
Askøy   Indre Arna
Straume   **Bergen**
Bergen Lufthavn   Norheimsund   Lofthus
Sotra   Flesland   Hardangerfjorden
Fana
Klokkarvik   Hardanger
Osøyri   Hårteigen   1690
Tyssedal
Odda
Hardangervidda

Snorre
Murchinson
Statfjord
Gullfaks
Veslefrikk
Troll
Oseberg
Brage

'I'm not from Norway. I'm from Bergen'.
This is how a native of Bergen shows that his town is a 'sovereign nation'. In the past, it was easier to sail to Britain and the Netherlands than to Oslo, so it is natural that Bergen has close links with the sea. This writer knows of <u>no other town which compares with Bergen.</u>
No-one ever passes through Bergen. Bergen is the final port of call on the traditional shipping routes across the North Sea. The Coastal Express and all the fjord routes terminate here. Naturally, after crossing the untamed mountains, railway lines from Vladivostok, St Petersburg, Stockholm and Oslo via the Bergensbanen line also terminate here. The same is true for the many roads blasted through the mountains with their tunnels and elegant bridges. Flights end in Bergen, no matter where they come from. Bergen is certainly no transit town.

Bergen - 'The Gateway to the Fjords'.
(Photo: Tourist Photo, Willy Haraldsen)

In the Middle Ages, Bergen was the vibrant centre of the Kingdom of Norway, which stretched from Ireland, the Orkney Islands, the Shetland Islands, the Faroe Islands and Iceland to Greenland. The bustling trading centre of the Hanseatic League in the North. Helicopter base for oil platforms in the North Sea. Each era has its own distinctive features. As is natural for the capital of the North Atlantic, Bergen has always faced west.

On our first day, we will be visiting this distinctive city. Our departure from Bergen is a thrilling start for the 4,000 km voyage. First some facts: 230,000 inhabitants. Area: 465 km². Three daily newspapers with a circulation of approximately 130,000. 1,958 mm rainfall per annum. 34 % of daylight period is sunshine. 3 million passengers pass through Flesland Airport every year. **The Tourist Information Office** is centrally situated on Fisketorget, in the same building as Den norske Bank and is open all year round. Pick up a free, detailed guide of Bergen here.

Location. The centre of the town is surrounded by **7 mountains**. The best known are **Fløien**, the summit of which can be reached on the **Fløibanen** funicular, and **Ulriken**, accessible by cable car. The town has spread out to the north, south and west. There are excellent and safe shipping routes to the southwest and the northwest.
According to historical sources, the town was established in 1070 by King Olav Kyrre. The original area of the town was small and centred around the **Vågen** area, where trade was concentrated. At the time, Trondheim (Nidaros) was the capital of Norway. However, in 1217, the great King Håkon Håkonson moved to Bergen and the town became the capital of the 'Kingdom of Norway'. The magnificent **Håkons Hall** was built at this time, as was the fortress, **Sverresborg.**

Today, it is difficult to imagine that Bergen was once the centre of political power and the bustling trading centre for the whole of the North Atlantic. Although the capital moved to Oslo in 1299, trade in Bergen continued, and the town grew to become Scandinavia's largest. The Hanseatic League established itself in 1350 and had a trade monopoly; a factor which was of decisive importance to the whole of coastal Norway, in particular to northern Norway. This monopoly lasted 200 years, and traders continued to move here after it ceased from the Netherlands and Germany. Shipping and trade flourished, and the town acquired a cosmopolitan character. Several impressive buildings were erected but, unfortunately, some of these were destroyed by fire, 1916 being a particularly bad year. However, the centre of the town has been rebuilt with wide streets and squares. A number of old buildings have been moved to **Gamle Bergen [Old Bergen]**, a small museum town, just outside Bergen. It is well worth a visit.

In addition to the traditional occupations, industry, commerce, administration and service industries have sprung up here. The production of oil in the North Sea has brought much activity with it (a large heliport is one example). **The University/School of Commerce** etc have expanded greatly.

Although there are a great many cultural events throughout the year, cultural life is characterised by the Bergen International Festival which is held from the end of May to early June. These events contribute greatly to the town's unique atmosphere and character, as do the historic buildings along the quays and Edvard Grieg's home, **Troldhaugen**, south of the centre of town. The **Bryggen** harbour area is included on UNESCO's heritage list of 89 international historic monuments.

Bergen's Bryggen district was the centre for trade with northern Norway and abroad. (Photo: Tourist Photo, Willy Haraldsen)

How shall we spend the day? We can recommend a sightseeing tour of the town which can be booked at the hotel or at the Tourist Information Office at Bryggen. You are certain to find something to your taste amongst the wide range of attractions on offer. 15 of these have been listed below:

1. **Akvariet [The Aquarium].** Europe's largest collection of salt water fish and other sea creatures.
2. **Bergenhus Festning [Bergenhus Castle]** which includes **Håkons Hall** and the **Rosenkrantz Tower.**
3. **Bergen Billedgalleri [Bergen Art Gallery], Stenersen Samlinger [the Stenersen Collection] and Rasmus Meyers samlinger [the Rasmus Meyer Collection].** Norwegian and foreign art.
4. **Bergens Sjøfartsmuseum [Bergen's Maritime Museum].**
5. **The Bryggen harbour area** and **The Hanseatic League Museum**.
6. **Bryggen Museum**. Artefacts from Bryggen. The world's largest collection of rune stones.
7. **Damsgård Hovedgård [Damsgård Estate].** Rococco building, furnishings and grounds. Open during the summer.
8. **Fiskerimuseet [Fishery Museum].** A cross-section of the fishing industry.
9. **Fisketorget [Fish Market].** Not open on Sundays.
10. **Gamle Bergen [Old Bergen].** Collection of 30 old houses.

11. **Historisk museum [Museum of History].** Ethnography. Cultural history.
12. **Lysøen, the home of the violinist and composer, Ole Bull,** outside the town. Open during the summer.
13. **Mariakirken,** Romanesque church dating from c. 1100. The town's oldest building.
14. **Schøttstuene.** Merchants 'club'.
15. **Troldhaugen,** the home of Edvard and Nina Grieg. Open during the summer. Troldsalen Hall with chamber concerts near to Troldhaugen.

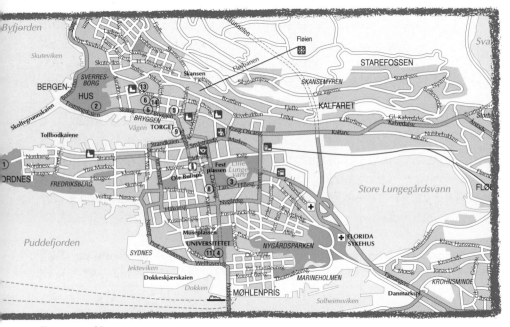

Town map of Bergen

You will board your Coastal Express with lasting memories of an interesting day in Bergen. The ship will be your home for the next eleven days on this non-stop sightseeing trip.

We begin our voyage by sailing westwards under the elegant **Askøy bridge**, Norway's 13th longest bridge, which measures 1,058 m in length. While you will see longer bridges along our route, this one has the longest single span in Norway - an amazing 850 m. Our route then turns to the north. **Askøy Island** to the east boasts old settlements and has 19,700 inhabitants. **The Øygarden chain of islands** to the west is linked by bridges. At Ågotnes lies a supply base for the North Sea oil fields. Oil is pumped through a sub-sea pipeline from the Oseberg field to the terminal at Sture. The characteristic "mushroom tower" can be seen when passing the terminal. Giant super-tankers load oil for export. Kollsnes, on the west side, is the site of the new terminal for natural gas, piped in from the Troll field. The community has 3,600 inhabitants. **The Hellesøy lighthouse** greets us and wishes us «good night». The next leg is described under day 12.

The voyage on the Coastal Express takes us on an 11 day non-stop tour in the waters of the Gulf Stream. Without it, the Norwegian coast would not have developed and would be underpopulated, just as Greenland, Labrador and Arctic Canada are. The fjords would be blocked by ice for several months in the winter.

The Gulf Stream arises at the point where the Equatorial Stream presses its warm water into the Caribbean, moving north into the Gulf of Mexico and then south past the southern tip of Florida. At this point it is 100 km wide and transports 25 million cubic metres of warm water eastward across the Atlantic ocean every second. Part of the stream continues north of the British Isles and approximately 4 million cubic metres per second turn in towards Norway, flowing along the entire coastline past the North Cape. It also flows into the fjords, ensuring that ports as far away as Murmansk in Russia remain free of ice all year round. During severe winters, ice sometimes forms in Kirkenes harbour.

Thanks to the Gulf Stream, 4.5 million people live in Norway. Fish have always flocked towards the coast in the same way as millions of sea birds do. (Naval commanders have always wished for ice-free ports in the deep fjords, where even the largest warships can anchor close to the side of the cliffs.

Say a word of thanks to the Gulf Stream every morning. Even if the weather Gods are not always on your side, you know that the stream is there, safeguarding the sea; the life-supporting environment of both humans and animals.

The fjord trip in to
Geiranger is only
included in the
summer season
schedule.

N
W · E
S

Ormen Lange

Smø

Grip Fyr

Grip

Sø

Kristiansund

Kvitholmen Fyr
Hustadvika
Atlanterhavsveien

Tus
Kvernberg

Averøya
Eide

Ona Fyr   Bjørnsund
Bud
Elnesvågen
ræna

Gossen

Hjelset

Molde lufthavn

Molde
Aukra
Langfjorden

Ei

Harøy

Fjørtoft
Flemsøya
Haramsøya
Lepsøya
Vigra
Valderøya
Giske Ålesund lufthavn
Godøy

Otrøy
Midsund
Romsdalsfjorden
Brattvåg
Søvik
Vatne
Vestnes
Veøy
Tomma

Andalsnes
Isfjorden

Romsdalshorne
1550

Ålesund
Spjelkavik
Skodje
Sjøholt

Langevåg
Sula
Hareid
Hjørungavåg
Sykkylven
Storfjorden

Fosnavåg
Herøy
Torvik
Ulsteinvik Vartdalsfjorden
Dolsteinshola
Gurskøy

Stordal

Stranda

Trollstigen

Romsda

Eike

Valldal

Tafjord

Vestkapp
Ervik
Stadlandet

Stadhavet

Runde

Svinøy Fyr

Nordlysfjorden

Ørsta
Volda

Hellesylt
Geiranger

Kråkenes Fyr
Einevarden
Skongenes Fyr
Selje
Kloster
Raudeberg
Vågsøy
Klovningen
Veststeinen Måløy

Nordfjord

Hornelen
Vingen

Nordfjordeid
Hjelmeset
Sandane

Stryn
Loen
Olden

Grotli

Bis

Lodalskåpa
2083

Galdhøpigg
2469

Frøya
Kalvåg Svelgen
Frøysjøen Botnane
Ålfotbreen

Hovden
Batalden
Stabben Fyr
Ytterøyane Fyr Skorpa
Kinn

Florø
Florø Lufthavn

Askrova
Svanøy
Stavenes
Fjærland
Fjordeidfjorden

Naustdal
Jølster

Jøstedalsbreen

Sognefjell

Jot
Na

Jølster

Atløy
Askvoll
Dale
Alden
Vilnesfjord
Korssund
Ospa
Gåsvær

Florø Førde
Førde Lufthavn

Fjærland

Gaupne

Store Skagastølstind
2403

Øvre Årdal

Utvær Fyr
Steinsund
Ytre Sula

Sula
Solund Kirke
Leirvik

Hyllestad
Vadheim Høyanger

Balestrand
Leikanger
Hermansverk
Sogndal
Kaupanger
Årdalstangen

Eivindvik

ognoksen

Holmengrå Fyr

Sognefjorden

Viksøyri

Lærdalsøyri

Fensfjorden
Vardøtangen
øy Fyr
Mongstad

Stølsheimen

Gudvangen Aurlandsvangen

As we round the West Cape, you'll have your first encounter with the ocean itself. This is where the Norwegian Sea opens up, providing a clear passage from here to America. After sailing for only 2 hours across the open Stadhavet sea, the route takes us through one of Norway's numerous island kingdoms which provide shelter both for the Coastal Express and the region's population. You are now as far west as Amsterdam and Marseilles but in 5 days we'll arrive at Vardø, which is on the same easterly longitude as St. Petersburg and Istanbul.

Hornelen (860 m above sea level) Early birds on board will catch sight of Hornelen mountain to the west. Legend has it that the great Viking king, Olav Trygvason, climbed to the top of this mountain. Every Christmas Eve and Midsummers Night (23 June) witches are said to gather on the mountain to dance with Old Nick. To the southeast, you can see mountains with a huge area of rock carvings depicting over 2,000 deer. Every year licences are granted to shoot 18,000 deer in Norway and 300-400 animals are killed in Bremanger alone.

Hornelen's jagged mountains evoke legends of the great climb and the witches' dance. (Photo: Knudsens Fotosenter)

MÅLØY (2,500 inhabitants. The municipality: 6,500 inhabitants)
One of Norway's largest fishing ports. Every year, 180,000-200,000 tonnes of fish are brought ashore here. Huge facilities for deep-freezing, drying cod, preserving etc. Direct exports abroad. Local paper with circulation of approximately 6,500. Statue of Captain Martin Linge who lost his life during the Allies' raid on Måløy on 17 December 1941. These attacks helped to convince Hitler that the invasion in Europe would take place in Norway. He used vast resources to build up the 'Festung Norwegen' defence system and stationed a considerable number of troops here. (May 1945: 360,000 men).

Måløy bridge is 1,224 m in length and has a clearance of 42 m. When the wind blows from a certain direction, the bridge produces its own 'high C' note.

Heading north, we pass Skorgenes lighthouse and Kråkenes lighthouse to the west. To the east, and not usually visible from the Coastal Express, lies Selje Monastery with its unique ruins. Legend has it that the beautiful Irish princess Sunniva escaped from her heathen suitor in a boat which had no oars. The boat was swept along by the Gulf Stream and ran aground here. When Håkon Jarl sent soldiers to the place, Sunniva and her companions fled into a large cave and she prayed for stones to block the entrance to the cave. She was later declared the patron saint of western Norway.

Måløy bridge is just one of the many magnificent bridges along the route, but is the only one to produce a 'high C' note. (Photo: Terje Hamre)

Stad/West Cape - Europe's arm in the Atlantic. The 500 m tall, 30 km long defiant mountain ridge is the dividing line for meteorologists' weather reports. For centuries, seafarers have associated the name with perilous journeys made with no protection from islands and skerries. A man-made ridge which is still visible today was used to haul lighter boats across the isthmus. This helped sailors to avoid many dangers and tragedies caused by storms which often surprised the 'convoys' which had gathered south and north of Stad in the hope of good weather.

Just south of the western tip, you'll see a small memorial chapel on a sandy beach. The place is called **Ervik**. The Coastal Express ship, St. Svithun, ran aground here on 30 September 1943 after Allied bombers accidentally attacked her. 45 people were killed. Several other ships and fishing boats have run aground here and many finds have been made on the beach, e.g. bronze Roman clasps and Anglo-Saxon silver coins.

Stad does not pose such a terrifying threat to today's ships and passengers. Most people enjoy witnessing the strength and charm of King Neptune, safe in the knowledge that the journey only takes around 2 hours. The **West Cape House** can be seen at the top of the 'Kjerringa' ['old lady'] mountain which towers 496 m over the ship.
North-east of Stad and to the east of our route, is Sandsøy Island, where Dolsteinshola is surrounded by a large number of Stone Age settlements. Further north, **Svinøy lighthouse** is to the west and the **Herøy Islands** are ahead of us. In this area the main industries are fishing and boat building. We pass by narrow straits, historical sites, ancient council sites and Herøy's burial ground where the bereaved had to supply sufficient earth to bury the deceased. The islands are linked together by such bridges as the 543 m long Herøy bridge.

TORVIK - Torvik is the Coastal Express' name for Herøy municipality's 8,500 inhabitants. Straight across the fjord one sees the municipal centre Ulsteinvik with 3,000 industrious inhabitants, fishing, shipbuilding and working in light engineering. On our way north, is **Runde,** western Norway's southernmost bird colony with some 1/2 million 'inhabitants'. Here there are at least 30 types of birds, (some say 200) among them puffins, kittiwakes, razorbills, common guillemots, cormorants, fulmars and gannets. A Dutch ship carrying 60,000 gold and silver coins sank here in 1725 - the coins were salvaged by divers in 1972.
ÅLESUND - (39,000 inhabitants - newspaper circulation: 38.000)
Floats on the sea and has lived off the sea. The town's fishing fleet operates from Greenland to the Barents Sea and provides the basis for an extensive fishing industry and fish exports. Ålesund is also the capital of Sunnmøre county and is populated by Norway's most hardworking people. There are factories or light engineering companies in each arm of the fjord.

Town map of Ålesund

The town burnt to the ground in 1904 and was rebuilt in the Art Nouveau style, which has largely been preserved. A trip to **Aksla mountain** in the middle of the town is a must. The view is spectacular. The town lies at your feet, clustered on islands and promontories. To the west you can see the open Atlantic Ocean and the islands with their ancient settlements. To the east are **'the Alps of Sunnmøre'** with their sharp peaks rising out of the fjord. British tourists began climbing here but the most well-known climber is William C. Slingsby, who, in 1876, conquered Kolåstind, 1,463 m above sea level.

The walkway made up of 418 steps, between the centre of the town and Aksla.Along the way you'll come across the statue of Rollon - Gange Rolv. He married the French king's daughter and founded the kingdom of Normandy. He is an ancestor of William the Conqueror, the British Royal Family . The statue was a present from Rouen, in France. We do not know for sure whether Gange Rolv was born in Ålesund or on the magnificent

Rollo

Ålesund burnt to the ground in 1904 and was rebuilt in the Art Nouveau style. (Photo: Tourist Photo, Willy Haraldsen)

island of Veøy in the Romsdals fjord, west of Molde. However, Queen Elizabeth can be proud of the fact that her predecessors came from such a beautiful district.

You will also find a statue of Kaiser Wilhelm II, the German emperor who visited the Norwegian fjords every summer until 1914, and who was quick to provide Ålesund with help after the fire in 1904.

Kaupangen lay on the east side of the town. The old trading centre **Borgund** lost its significance when the Hanseatic League acquired exclusive trade rights. Today, you can visit a charming museum here, with boats and an Arctic section as well as a church from the mid thirteenth century. There is an aquarium in the centre of town with many species of fish from the North Sea and Norwegian Sea. And last - but not least - Ålesund is an excellent place for shopping.

The Geiranger Fjord.
The pearl of the West Country fjords.

But what is a fjord?

Fjords are a trademark of tourism in Norway. When the glaciers receded from the land-mass towards the coast, they carved great valleys through the mountain ranges. The ice deposited vast thresholds of rocks at the coast, which formed barriers against the cold waters of the deeps outside, but allowed the warmer surface water to pass over into the fjords. The fjords are normally free from ice during the winter. The marine environment meets soaring mountains with fertile valleys and vegetation clinging to crevices and sheer cliffs. There are few places around the globe where this combination of mild marine climate, severe mountain terrain and mainland culture meet so uniquely.

Tourism started in the 19th century with salmon fishing, the king among fish, and mountain climbing among the peaks and pinnacles of the mountains that soar almost vertically from the seas and fjords. Car and cruise ship tourism came much later.

Royal personages from Great Britain and The Netherlands - and not least the German Kaiser - were regular visitors, and had personal acquaintances amongst the local inhabitants. The fjords have many idyllic, picturesque and memorable venues to offer, but the Coastal Express has chosen the cruise metropolis Geiranger as the representative of the inshore coastal countryside.

The fjord reaches more than 100 km from Ålesund to Geiranger. (Norway's longest fjord is Sognefjorden, 204 km long.) The first stretch is typified by lively small towns and villages. On the fjord's north bank, Sula (7000 inhabitants) has refused amalgamation with Ålesund and is full of energy and initiative. On the south bank lies what was once the centre for seal hunting in the Arctic. Further east along the south bank lie Sykkylven and Ekornes, major furniture industry centres. Can it be the area's natural beauty that inspires the 7,000 inhabitants to produce goods for the world's markets? (Perhaps you've heard of Stressless?)

The mid section of the fjord is typified by the high mountains that strive to keep the sea at bay. It's impossible for mere mortal beings to build their towns here, with the exception of the country town of Stranda (the community has 4,600 inhabitants), which started the furniture industry. The town then started with sausage production and has recently also developed a pizza-industry.

The inner reaches of the fjord is the total domain of the mountains, which allow only a few drops of Atlantic water to reach their feet. Everything that happens here is on the mountains' premises. You can't help but admire the stout souls who established the tiny mountainside farms far above you. The tax collector couldn't always manage the climb to deliver his demand, the pathway up was so steep that in places ladders were installed. And it happened that the ladders had been taken away "for repairs" when the tax collector was out on his errands. It was different when Queen Sonja and King Harald celebrated their silver wedding at one of the farms, together with many foreign guests. The Queen took the traditional route up, but many of the guests preferred to take the helicopter! Here you will also see (provided there's been enough rain) "Brudesløret og de syv søstre" - the Bride's Veil and the Seven Sisters – who dance playfully down the mountain in youthful joy while the manly "Friaren" – Courtier - flirts with them from the far side of the fjord. At the very end of the fjord lies the idyllic agricultural village that has become the favourite venue of the world's cruise operators. A modern adventure and experience centre has been built here, but we don't have enough time to stop and visit now. It is however er our hope that you will gather up all your impressions of Geiranger and keep them safely in your heart. We believe that you will remember the nine hours you spent on the Coastal Express in the Geirangerfjord with great joy and pleasure, and the knowledge that you have had an unforgettable experience.

The Geirangerfjord is a classic attraction, and has received innumerable visits from international cruise ships.

Giske - As we leave Ålesund, we pass true Viking territory to the west. Giske Island was ruled by great chieftains. Tora from Giske gave birth to two princes, and the family owned up to 200 farms and were involved in the fishing and shipping industries, carrying out a considerable amount of trade. Imagine the wealth of this district in the Middle Ages. Nevertheless, its inhabitants travelled to England, Scotland and Ireland to trade - trips which became pillaging and looting raids. Women often returned with the men, though few people believe that they did so of their own accord. The Vikings brought Christianity back with them - the marble church at Giske being evidence of this. The settlement, however, does date back further than this. Finds from the late Stone Age have been made in Skjonghelleren - a large cave on the west side of the island, **Valderøya** - and in several burial mounds.

The Coastal Express passes over one of Norway's many subsea tunnels, the 4,200 m long tunnel to Valderøya. From here, bridges and a tunnel lead from Ålesund to Giske and **Godøy** and to **Vigra** airport, which handles over 650,000 passengers every year. The island municipality has 6,300 inhabitants.

Towards the east we see **Brattvåg** (2,000 inhabitants). The town is a hive of industry, with strong ties to the production of shipping equipment, fishing boats and the fish processing industry. Car ferries to the outer islands dock in the bustling harbour. Eventually, we turn east towards Romsdals Fjord. Many active centres of fishing and industry can be found along both sides of the fjord. We'll drop anchor here at the very heart of **Romsdalen** , right in the centre of **MOLDE** - Town of the Roses.

Facing south, the town is sheltered by the mountains in the north. The view over the wide fjord has made the town famous. The mouth of the fjord is to the west, but islands and skerries provide shelter from storms and the sea climate. The fjord widens

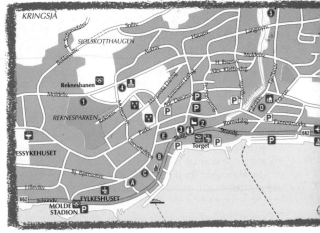

Town map of Molde

as it proceeds south towards the **Alps of Romsdalen** - 87 snow-clad peaks. To the east, the fjord narrows, forging its way between the mountains as far as **Åndalsnes** and **Trollstigveien.** This area is a paradise for mountain climbers and salmon fishermen, as Trollveggen is to parachutists. The Alps may well be magnificent, but Romsdalens' mountains plunge straight into the sea. The salty water and the smell invoke an atmosphere lacking in inland lakes.

Molde has a clear view across the fjord to the alps of Romsdalen. (Photo: Knudsens Fotosenter)

MOLDE rises up above the slope, enabling its 23,000 inhabitants to savour the view every day. This quality of life also raises the standard of living.

Varden, a view point 407 m above sea level, towers over the settlement. The town was blitzed in 1940 and 2/3 of it was destroyed. During the bombing, a famous picture was taken of the King and Crown Prince taking cover under a birch tree which is now known as **'Kongebjerka'**.

Therefore much of the settlement, including the magnificent cathedral, dates from the 1950s. Beautiful farms lie outside the town. Horse chestnuts, maples, holly, linden, ash and copper beech grow here in happy ignorance of the fact that this is the northerly limit for these types of tree. Molde is home to industries such as furniture making and the production of lighting fixtures. The fishing industry was situated to the west. Today, the town is an administrative and trade centre, as well as tourist town. It also has educational facilities to university level. The airport caters for over 300,000 passengers every year. Three of Norway's greatest writers have links with the town. The Nobel prize winner, Bjørnstjerne Bjørnson went to school here (and studied the Snorre legends). Ibsen vacationed here and often stayed at the beautiful rococo farm Moldegård, which you will see east of the town (" Rosmersholm" was probably written here). Kielland lived here as the district governor (a statue was erected in his memory). Today, the annual jazz festival is the town's best-known cultural event. Newspaper circulation: 19,000

Continuing north from Molde, the Coastal Express passes **Julsundet.** On the mainland, the productive municipality of **Fræna** (9,000 inhabitants) has strong ties with industry, fishing and farming. To the west, **Gossen Island** is as flat as a pancake (Aukra municipality has 3,000 inhabitants). We are now heading for **Hustadvika.** The abandoned fishing village **Bjørnsund** lies to the west. Its population is supported by holidaymakers who visit during the summer. The school is used as a holiday school for children from all over the country.

Bud, a traditional fishing village with 800 inhabitants is situated on the mainland. Its wooden church dates back to 1717. It also has a monument to the so-called "National Council" of 1533 when the catholic archbishop, Olav Engelbrektsson, tried in vain to declare Norway's independence from the Danish king. As the German coastal fort was below the memorial, it meant that the church tower lay in the line of fire and had to be demolished. It was later rebuilt.

We are now in Hustadvika which, on the map, looks like a part of the open sea. It is in fact a 3 km wide belt of small islands and skerries where even the most experienced pilot is dependent on buoys and sea marks to find his way. This is a paradise for sport divers, with luxurious sea plants and rare types of algae. (And maybe an old shipwreck full of gold) The coastal waters are so dangerous that the route of the Coastal Express lies further out. Countless stone graves are evidence of former settlements. The Hustadir royal estate was situated here and this is where King Øystein Magnussen died in 1122. Today, large areas are newly cultivated and are more reminiscent of the Po Plain in Italy than Norway's mountainous countryside.

In the evening, **Kvitholmen lighthouse** can be seen to the west and the **Atlantic Ocean Road** to the east. This impressive feat of engineering spans 8 low bridges crossing small islands and skerries in the mouth of the fjord. Key West, the famous system of bridges in Florida, seems like a toy compared to this road which appears to defy nature. Centres for divers and sports fishermen are to be found 10 km further north and beyond **Averøya Island** (5,400 inhabitants). You can help yourself to the sea's riches without having to offer up a fisherman's prayer or know much about fishing. Sea fishing is free to everyone. A seaside house and a restored fishing village on **Håholmen** have sleeping accommodation available to fishermen, if they wish to take advantage of it. Here the adventurer Ragnar Thorseth reigns. See the Viking ship he used on his many journeys. After night falls, the Coastal Express heads for **Kristiansund** (described under day 11). Kristiansund will also be visited on the return journey.

The Norwegian coast has always provided a rich source of food for sea birds. Throughout history there have been periods of "black sea" when the capelin and herring have more or less disappeared, severely affecting the bird population. The damage to the spring spawning herring as a result of overfishing in the 1960s led to a serious lack of herring fry along the coast of North Norway for nearly 20 years. During the late 1980's and early 1990's Capelin stocks in the Barents Sea were catastrophically depleted. Feeding conditions have since improved, but the sea bird populations that were affected have not recovered. In the northern counties the nesting populations of the common guillemot, which was halved during the capelin crisis, has been reduced by more than 90% since the 1960s. This tragic situation was not improved by birds which drown in fishing nets and as a result of the increase in oil pollution. The lack of herring fry at Røst meant that puffins in the area have had long term problems with finding enough food for their offspring, and the large population has been reduced by 70% since 1979. The Norsk institutt for naturforskning [Norwegian Institute for Scientific Research] has released the following figures for the largest bird colonies. Altogether the figures in the table represent around 80% of the total Norwegian nesting population of sea birds. Even if only six of these bird colonies lie along the last leg of the Coastal Express' journey, Honningsvåg-Kirkenes, you will still be able to see hundreds of thousands of other sea birds en route, and you will pass extremely close to a colony at Sværholtklubben. Notice that the figures show nesting pairs of birds. The actual number of birds in the colonies is more than twice the figures shown.

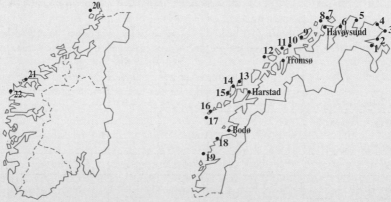

Approximate number of nesting pairs of the most common species of sea bird in the largest bird colonies along the coast. Colonies of less than 100 pairs arc not shown. Source: Det nasjonale sjøfuglkartet, NINA (unpublished), The Norwegian Institute for Scientific Research (NINA), table: Jan Eivind Østnes, text: Tycho Anker-Nilssen.

Colony	Fulmar Fulmarus glacialis	Gannet Sula bassana	Kittywake Rissa tridactyla	Razorbill Alca torda	Common guillemot Uria aalge	Brünnich's guillemot Uria lomvia	Puffin Fratercula arctica
1. Ranvika			10.000				
2. Store Ekkerøy			15.-20.000				
3. Hornøy			20.000	200	4.000	500	8.000
4. Syltefjord		500	150.000	200	1.350	100	100
5. Omgangstauran			75.000		500		
6. Sværholtklubben			40.-50.000				
7. Gjesværstappan		1000	1.500	3.-4.000	400	200	400.000
8. Hjelmsøy			50.000	10.000	1.200	800	60.000
9. Andotten			5.000				
10. Loppa			300	2.-4.000	350		15.000
11. Nord-Fugløy				1.-2.000	100		200.000
12. Sør-Fugløy				1-500	100		185.000
13. Bleiksøy			6.000	100	250		80.000
14. Anda			800				25.000
15. Nykvåg			4.000	250	200		180.000
16. Værøy			25.000	800	500		50.000
17. Røst	3-500		15.000	1.-3.000	500		450.000
18. Fugløy				1.-5.000			10.000
19. Lovunden							50.000
20. Sklinna					200		5.000
21. Runde	5.000	1.800	40.-50.000	2.-3.000	8.000		50.-100.000
22. Veststeinen					100		8.000

Puffin. 30 cm. Nests in colonies on the coast from Rogaland and further north. (Photo: Johannes Jensås)

Kittywake. 41 cm. Nests in colonies on the coast from Rogaland and further north. (Photo: Johannes Jensås)

Gannet. 90 cm. Nests on Runde off Ålesund and in four colonies in north Norway. (Photo: Viggo Ree)

Razorbill. 41 cm. Nests in colonies in the outer skerries from Utsira and further north. (Photo: Viggo Ree)

Common guillemot. 42 cm. Nests in colonies on the coast from Rogaland and further north. (Photo: Johannes Jensås)

Brünnich's guillemot. 42. cm. Nests in colonies in northern Norway, and also on Runde. (Photo: Viggo Ree)

Fulmar. *47 cm. Nests along the Norwegian coast from Rogaland to Finnmark. (Photo: Johannes Jensås)*

Grey Gull. *60 cm. Nests along the entire coast and at certain inland sites. (Photo: Viggo Ree)*

Red billed tern. *35 cm. Nests along the entire coast and also inland. (Photo: Viggo Ree)*

Eider duck. *58 cm. Nests along the entire Norwegian coast. (Photo: Viggo Ree)*

Cormorant. *76 cm. Nests in colonies from Rogaland to Finnmark. (Photo: Viggo Ree)*

Sea eagle. *70-90 cm. Nests in coastal areas from Rogaland to Finnmark. (Photo: Johannes Jensås)*

N
W E
S

Heidrun
Åsgard
Kristin
Lavrans
Tyrihans
Mikkel

Draugen
Njord

HALTENBANKEN

VELFJORDEN

SKLINNABANKEN

Sklinna Fyr

Horta

Nordøyan Fyr

Vikna

Lysøya

Leka
Solsemhulen
Fingarshulen
Risvær
Gjerdinga

Cutvik

Foldereid

Terråk

Vennesund
Holm

Bindalsfjorden
Tosenfjorden

Fyingen
Tilrem
Skåren
Brønnøysund
Torghatten
Trolnes
Berg
Hølmestø
Tos
Sømna

Indre Foldafjorden

Rørvik
Ottersøy
Nærøy
Nærøysundet
Gjæslingan Fyr
Abelvær

Kolvereid

Salsbruket

Foldfjorden

Folda

Ellingsråsa Fyr

Kya Fyr

Jøa
Aglen
Utvorda

Dun

Namdalen

Høylandet

E6

Namsenfjorden

Lauvsnes

Buholmråsa Fyr

Flatanger

Namsos

Skage
Bergsmo

Rånemsletta

Grong

Sandvikberget

Bangsund

Namsen

Hepsøya
Osen

Namdalseid

Snåsa

Kaura Fyr
Bessaker
Værøya
Roan

Finnvær Fyr

Froan

Harbakhulen
Harsvik
Stokksund
Stokkøya
Linesøya
Åsenvågøy Fyr
Afjord

Velde

Malm

Sunnan

E6

FROHAVET

Vingleia Fyr

Mausund

Lysøysund

FOSENHALVØYA

Foldafoss

Steinkjer

Mære
Sparbu
Straumen

Beitstadfjorden

Tarva Fyr

Kjeungskjær Fyr

Botngård

Austrått
Råkvagen

Verdalsøra

Sistranda
Hammarvika
Storfosna
Uthaug
Brekstad

Frøya

Fillan
Hestvika
Sandstad

Hitra

Jøsnøya
Hemskjel
Tjeldbergodden

Ørlandet
Agdenes Fyr
Rissa
Reinskloster
Lensvik
Sellbekken

Leksvik

Vannvikan

Levanger
Skogn

Frosta

Åsen

E6

Trondheimsfjorden

Trondheim

Malvik

Skatval
Værnes

Stjørdalshalsen

Hegra

Kyrksæterøra

Gjølme
Børsa

Heimdal
Hommelvik

Trondheim Lufthavn

Midtbygda
Kopperå

Orkanger

Klæbu
Melhus

Selbu

Orkdal
Svorkmo
Løkken
Storås

Kvål
Ler
Lundamo
Hovin

E6

Rindal
Meldal
Aa

Støren

dalsøra

GAULDALEN

Nidaros, now Trondheim, was Norway's first capital city and is situated at the mouth of the River Nid. (After fierce conflict, a majority of the population have rejected the original name). Fertile communities lined the shores of the long, wide Trondheims Fjord and agriculture, forestry, fishing and hunting provided excellent living standards. The area was governed by popularly elected local chieftains, and it was the port of departure for Viking expeditions. Many a Viking ship was dragged onto the sandy banks of the river Nid for trade or festivities after an expedition. The chieftain's men (bodyguards) were the finest of men. Leiv Eriksson completed his military service here before returning home to Greenland (which at the time was part of the Norwegian territory). Torfinn Karlsefni also docked here, after the long expedition to Leiv Eriksson's home in Vinland (Newfoundland). He brought home timber from 'the new country' which he sold to a merchant from Bremen. The first ever export of American goods to Europe took place here around 1000 AD. (Source: Snorre and Adam von Bremen).

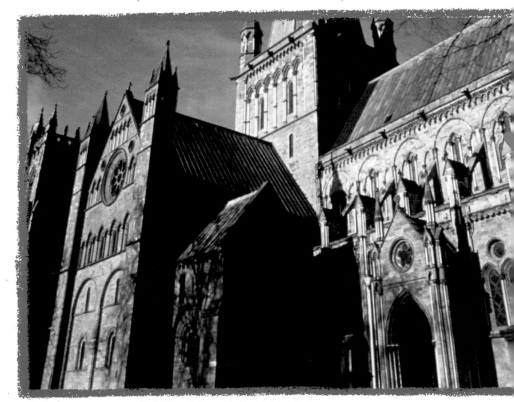

Trondheim (Nidaros) lies at the heart of central Norway and was Norway's capital when the country was unified.
(Foto: Nancy Bundt)

By this time, however, the people of Trøndelag had already defeated all Norway's local chieftains in great sea battles, thus unifying Norway in 872 AD. Nidaros remained the capital until 'the imperialist' Håkon Håkonsson moved to Bergen in 1217. During these years, Trondheim developed into Norway's religious centre. It began with the death of St Olav at the battle of Stiklestad in 1030. Pilgrims came from far and wide to be healed at St. Olav's shrine in Nidaros. The town became the seat of the archbishop in 1152 and continued to be Norway's ecclesiastical centre until the Reformation in 1533. In the 11th century, a church was built over the holy shrine of St. Olav, and it remained one of Europe's most important places of pilgrimage until the Reformation. The church was damaged by fire several times. Swedish troops conquered the town twice, but the white Kristiansten fortress was not captured. Restoration work started on the cathedral in 1869, and has continued until the present day. Nidaros Cathedral is now of great national and cultural importance in Norway, and is one of northern Europe's greatest Gothic memorials. The Museum of Music History at Ringve is another unique place which is well worth visiting in Trondheim. Victoria Bachke, a Russian artist who fled from the Revolution in St. Petersburg and married in Trondheim, used her energy and special charm to collect musical instruments from a large number of countries. This resulted in a rare collection of items from all over the world and from different eras in the history of music.

In addition to Nidaros Cathedral, Trondheim is also the home of the fascinating Ringve Museum of Music History. (Photo: Knudsens Fotosenter)

Architecturally, Trondheim is a town of wooden buildings such as Singsaker Studenthjem [Singsaker student hall]. Stiftsgården [the Stiftsgården palace] is Scandinavia's second largest wooden building. The harbour buildings along the River Nid and the Town Bridge are also well worth a visit. There are plenty of salmon in the river. After the fire in 1681, Johan Casper von Cicignon from Luxembourg drew up plans for the town and lay the foundations for the present settlement. For generations, Norges Tekniske Høyskole [University of Trondheim] has educated civil engineers (who have seduced the female population of the town into becoming their wives and moving to all corners of the country). Norway's largest research institute (SINTEF) is also located here. Cultural life is rich (Trøndelag Theatre and the concert hall, Olavshallen, The Museum of Music History at Ringve, chamber orchestra etc.).

A few facts:
149,000 inhabitants. Area: 342 km². Cultivated land: 73 km². Forests: 122 km². Newspapers: Adresseavisen, circulation 88,000. 34% of daylight period is sunshine. 2.1 million passengers pass through Værnes, Trondheim's airport, every year (i.e. 14 times the town's population).

What to do in Trondheim?
1. **Nidaros Cathedral.**
2. **Musikkhistorisk museum [Museum of Music History]** at Ringve. Open 20 May - 30 September.
3. **Stiftsgården palace.** Open June-August.
4. **Vitenskapsmuseet [Science Museum].**
5. **Trøndelag Folkemuseum [Trøndelag Folk Museum].** Open May-August.
6. **Trondheim Kunstforening [Trondheim Art Association].** Closed on Mondays.

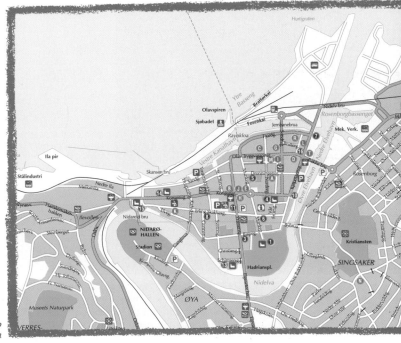

Town map of Trondheim

Our departure from Trondheim is undramatic. To the east, we catch a glimpse of Trøndelag county's widespread communities - the majestic fjord and the birthplace of Norway's political history. However, the Coastal Express concentrates on the coast itself and we therefore head west.

Just outside the town, we pass the islet of **Munkholmen.** Its monastery dates back to the Middle Ages and was damaged by fire. A fort was built in the 17th century, but it was never of any military significance. Its cannons were not large enough to ward off the Swedes who conquered Trondheim in 1658 and 1718. When a German warship entered the harbour on 9 April 1940, the town had neither guns nor shells with which to defend itself. Today, Munkholmen is a popular bathing and leisure destination on sunny days. Listen to stories of the great Danish politician, Griffenfelt, who was imprisoned here for 18 years.

Historical Munkholmen is a decorative, but insignificant sentry post for the capital of Trøndelag.
(Photo: Samfoto, Jon Arne Sæter)

On our way out of the fjord, we see a large bay to the south. This bay was the setting for Sigrid Undset's novels about Kristin Lavransdatter. Orkanger, a large industrial area, is also to be found here. Next, we see the farming community of Lensvik and Agdenes lighthouse (closed down) and the former Agdenes fortress.

North of the Fosen peninsula are areas well-known from Johan Bojer's novels. Further, the large farm Reinskloster, historically famous in Norway, and Fosen Mek. Verksted, [Fosen Shipyard] shipbuilders, who built among others the Coastal Express vessels M/S Trollfjord and M/S Midnatsol. Directly north, and not visible from the ship, is Austrått, the home of 'Fru Inger', one of Norway's most influential women in the 1500s. Her 16th century castle burned to the ground, but has now been partly restored. An eerie German coastal defence battery guards the approach to Trondheims Fjord. The artillery comprises a gun tower from the German battleship Gneisenau which was destroyed by bombs. The gun tower was saved and towed to Austrått where it is now a modern attraction. Further out, near the mouth of the fjord, we pass the administrative centre of Brekstad (4,900 inhabitants). The local newspaper has a circulation of 6,800. Each year a 'Partisans March' is held to commemorate the Serbian prison camp which was located here during World War II.

Storfosna Island, with its large estates, lies to our west as we head directly north and away from Trondheims Fjord. To the east is Ørlandet air station, built as a NATO base after 1950. The station is the base for large air-sea rescue helicopters. Agricultural areas have been expanded through the construction of dams and a canal leading to the sea, and in this way the land lost to the air station was compensated for. The lighthouse at Kjeungskjær welcomes us as we approach Frohavets multitude of skerries.

Travelling northwards, we see a myriad of smaller islands and skerries and the rich Frøya and Halten fishing banks to the west. The Halten bank has recently become a familiar term in the oil industry, and its large gas fields are now coming on stream. A long pipeline stretching southwards to Tjeldbergodden (see Day 11) leads to the ammonia purification plant and export harbour.

A gas fired power station is being constructed at Skogn / Levanger amongst the other industries already established there. The gas pipe from Haltenbanken was laid along the bed of the Trondheimsfjord to Skogn.

The Norwegian coastline has 30,000 islands, at least 100,000 skerries and millions of birds, but how many mountains? (Photo: Per Eide)

For centuries, a typical feature of Norway's coastal communities has been the combination of farming and fishing. In addition to local inshore fishing, fishing boats often ventured far out to sea for seasonal fishing. Imagine journeying from here to Lofoten and back to take part in the rich winter cod fishing! Try fishing yourself in one of the special Åfjord boats for which this stretch of coast is so famous. These boats are extremely seaworthy because, in the past, fishermen could not always swim!

The most prosperous times for the district were when the herring swam into the fjords to spawn. That was a real adventure! If herring stocks are allowed to grow, this time may return. You may possibly prefer fishing for salmon in one of the many excellent inland salmon rivers. The writer of this brochure can recommend fish farming, which has become a new branch of industry. Do not be fooled into thinking that you will be able to succeed at this without the appropriate qualifications. It may, however, prove a new source of income.

We pass **Stokksund** during the late afternoon. At this point, you will understand the importance of good sea charts and the art of navigation. When Kaiser Wilhelm II of Germany sailed into this area, he became so nervous that he took the wheel himself. The pilot, Nordhus, managed to get rid of him with the words 'I'm the boss here' - he was later given a gold watch by the repentant Kaiser.

The large mountain caves at Stokksund and Osen (further north) may have once provided shelter for outlaws. The largest of these is Halvikhulen cave, which widens to reveal a large hall, 100 metres from the entrance.

The Coastal Express does not have time to dock at the timber and salmon town of Namsos, 40 km into the fjord, but continues straight ahead across Folda. In 2 1/2 hours time, we will be heading across this open stretch of sea towards the large island kingdom of Vikna in the north. This is the setting for Olav Duun's work. To the west, lighthouses flash over the fishing grounds and the newly discovered wealth from the oil and gas fields. Kjetil Hæng, an ancestor of the saga writer Snorre Sturlason, lived in the north. This provides the basis for a philosophical evening. But of course you can take a stroll when we tie up at Rørvik, and visit the Norveg National Centre for Coastal Culture. If you prefer, you can wait until we're on the southbound leg, when you'll have more time at your disposal. (see description of Day 10). Tomorrow, the day begins at the Arctic Circle - this promises to be an extremely eventful day.

THE ARCTIC CIRCLE

Early in the morning, we cross the Arctic Circle, the border with the Land of the Midnight Sun. This invisible border circles the earth at 66° 33' north, marking the southernmost point at which the Midnight Sun shines 24 hours a day on Midsummer Night's Eve. This occurs 23° 27' from the North Pole, due to the angle between the sun's orbit and the earth's orbit at the Equator. The earth's axis is tilted towards the sun. Scientists have calculated the exact dates of the solstice - 21 June and 21 December. You will be able to check the place for yourself. To the west, you can see Hestmannen Island. To the east, and at the point where the Svartisen glacier rises towards the sky, Mel Fjord cuts 30 km inland. A globe has been built on a small island - Vikingen - just west of the route, which is visible during the day. Even if you don't see the border, the captain will make sure that the occasion is a memorable event. From then on, you belong to the same family as 400,000 of Norway's citizens who, for centuries, have been members of the world's northernmost civilisation.

The sun reaches its lowest point on 22 December, and is on a tangent to the Arctic Circle. By the next day, it has already started to move, slowly but surely, northwards again. Throughout January, the sun will be above the horizon across all of northern Norway. However, even when the sun is not above the horizon, days are not in total darkness. Days are usually characterised by dusk and twilight, with a clear flicker of light spread across the sky. The mountains are covered in glistening white snow, the Northern Lights flood the scenery and the moon does its best to shine its brightest.

N
W   E
S

Kvæfjord

Straume
Bø
Litløy Fyr
Vesterålsfjorden
Sørland
Kleiva
Flesnes
Revsnes
Sigerfjord
Skagen
H n n ø y a
Kongs

Hadseløya
Stokmarknes
Møysalen
*1262
Melbu
Hadsel

Hadselfjorden
Lødingen
Ofotfjorden

Eggum
Gimsøy
Austvågøy
Trollfjorden

Svolvær Lufthavn
Svolvær
Brettesnes
Tranøy Fyr

Vestvågøy
Vågakallen
942 *
Kabelvåg
Skrova Fyr
Hamsund
Hamarøy
Øk

Flakstadøy
Leknes
Henningsvær
Moholmen Fyr

Fredvang
Gravdal
Ure
Stamsund

Ramberg
Mortsund
Skutvik

Ballstad
Henningsværstraumen

Sund
Nusfjord
Nesland

Mølnarodden
Hamnøy
Flatøy Fyr
Sagfjorden
Tysfjorden

Moskenes
Reine
Engeløya

Tind
Sørvågen
Grøtøy

Å
Steigen
Leinesfjorden

Moskenesstraumen
Skarholmen Fyr
Måløy
Leiranger

VESTFJORDEN

Værøy
Sørland
Folda

Værøy Fyr

Nykan
Røst
Røsthavet
Kjerringøy
Sørfolda
E6

Skomvær Fyr
Rago
Nasjonalpark

Heligvær
Landegode Fyr
Røsvik

Salten
Straumen

Tennholmen Fyr
Bliksvær
Bodø

Bodø Lufthavn
Løding
Strømsnes
Fauske

Kjerstadfjorden
Saltstraumen
Saltfjorden

Suliskon
*
1907

Arnøy
Sandhornøy
Gildeskål Kirke
Sulithjelma

Fugløya
Inndyr
Rognan

Tennholmfjorden
Høgnakken
Beiarn
E6

VØRINGBASSENGET
Kunna
1045

Kalsholmen Fyr
Støtt
Saltdalen

Ørnes
Meløy
Myken Fyr
Glomfjord

Bølga
Grønøy

Amøy
Saltfjellet
Nasjonalpark

Holandsfjorden

Rødøyløva
440 *
Engabreen

Ringsundøya
Istind
*
1572

Nesøya
Gjerøya
Snøtind
*
1599
Svartisen

Træna
Hestmannøy
568 *
Hestmona

RÆNABANKEN
Træna Fyr
Lurøy
POLARSIRKELEN

Trænfjorden

Lovunden
Lurøy
Stroforshei
E6

Lovunden
Lovund
Krigskirkegård

Åsvær Fyr

Tømma
Utskarpen
Mo i Rana

Dønnes kirke Nesna
Ranafjorden
Hemnesberget

LOFOTEN

Legend has it that **Hestmann Island**, originally **Hestmona** (568 m above sea level), was formed when a knight was turned to stone as he forgot the sunrise because of his intense love for the woman Lekamøya. It is said that he shot an arrow at Lekamøya which passed through the hat of a troll further south. He is clearly visible from the ship, as is the hole in Torghatten Mountain, which you will see on the trip south, Day 10. Climbers need ropes to get from Hestmannen's neck to the peak which is as flat as a pancake.

Hestmann Island is located on the Arctic Circle. (Photo: Espen Bratlie)

Most islands along the route have been inhabited for generations, but, in recent times, there has been a large-scale exodus from former fishing villages to larger islands and towns. This has partly been funded by the state. To the west is Rødøy church which, at the time when people rowed to church on Sundays, was a meeting point for people from surrounding islands and fishermen who often lived in remote areas close to the fishing grounds. Today, the municipality of Rødøy has 1,500 inhabitants and an administrative centre which is located further inland on the mainland.

Rødøyløva [The Red Lion Rock], to the west of the Coastal Express' route, resembles an enigmatic Egyptian Sphinx. The countryside is different, but Rødøyløva's 444 m high head indicates that this is the land of living adventure, in contrast to the desert's ancient hidden treasures.

DAY 4. THE ARCTIC CIRCLE - STAMSUND......

Svartisen Glacier lights up the land to the east. It is Norway's second largest glacier (only Jostedals Glacier between Sogne Fjord and Nord Fjord is larger). Inland peaks rise 1,500 m above sea level, the highest being Snøtind (1,599 m above sea level).

Svartisen Glacier is best seen from the sea. Many people enjoy studying the cold mystery of the ice and the glacier for themselves.
(Photo: Aune Forlag)

To the east, there are large caves in the limestone mountains and superb marked trails for ramblers. In the fjord itself, the glacier's 'fingers' once stretched all the way to the shore. Modern cruise ships sail into Holands Fjord to view a large finger of the Enga Glacier which stretches across the entire breadth of the fjord. Melt water from the glacier provides Norsk Hydro with cheap hydro-electric power for its large factory in Glomfjord (1,250 inhabitants). These factories produce calcium nitrate, ammonia and enough chemical fertilizer for the whole of Norway. New products are taking shape in a new industrial park. Today, melt water is collected *under* the glacier and channelled through 45 tunnels into one huge tunnel leading to a power station at the coast. The aim is to exploit every inch of the drop without intruding on nature.

A good main road (Kystriksvei 17) now runs the length of the coastline between Trondheim and Bodø. Several fjords must still be crossed by car ferries, but the crossings are relatively short.

Grøn Island is a surprisingly green and fertile island to the east. In the 18th century, it was a trading centre and, from 1778, housed an inn. It was once a port of call for the Coastal Express. To the west you can see the unique formation of Bolga Island.

North of our route is **Mel Island**, once the home of the aristocratic Benestok family who, in the 16th century, owned large properties between here and Bodø.

ØRNES, 1,500 inhabitants. A port of call for the Coastal Express, Ornes has a popular beach. The municipality has 6,800 inhabitants. As it is the centre for local boat services, you'll often see the modern high speed vessels which cater for local traffic. Ørnes was a prosperous place of trade in 1794. In spite of fires which have ravaged the town, period houses dating back to the 1800s can still be seen.

All along the coast, you'll find former trading posts which remain untouched by progress. Around 1700, and in accordance with national plans, places of trade were set up all along the coast. Fish from northern Norway was an important commodity and Bergen was the export harbour. In conjunction with this, the authorities granted innkeepers licenses for places which had natural advantages, and which often lay within a day's travel of each other.

The people of the North were completely dependent on transport to Bergen. Many stories have been told of why it was so vital for the fish to be exported via the merchants of Bergen. This gave rise to a considerable amount of coastal traffic during the spring and autumn, with local freight vessels carrying goods back to the local communities. Fishermen were often extremely dependent on the local merchant, since he purchased the catch for further sale and, at the same time, sold imported essentials. Many fishermen fell into debt with the traders, who often owned the entire fishing village. Fishing village owners were hated by many, but history has proven that the merchant was actually a vital member of the community. Most of these merchants had a certain understanding of the fishermens' problems. Several of them left behind buildings of vast cultural and historical importance. The best known of these is on the island, Kjerringøy, north of Bodø. It has been completely restored and is popular with tourists. You will not often see places such as this from the Coastal Express. These places live a Sleeping Beauty-like existence, far removed from the rest of the world.

Kunna boasts a large number of findings from Iron Age settlements. The island is now linked to the mainland, but in former times boats could pass between the island and the mainland. To the west is the former trading post of Støtt. Among the many ships which have run into difficulty in these waters is the Norwegian submarine 'Uredd', which sank just north of here during a mission to occupied Norway in World War II . The island of **Fugleøy** to the west is home to a large colony of puffins.

Gildeskål church on the mainland can usually be seen from the Coastal Express. It was built by King Øystein in 1130, probably on an old heathen site. The new church, Nykirken, dating back to 1881, is nearby. The feudal overlords of the counties in the north resided at Inndyrgodset estate from 1604. Just north lies Sandhornøy Island and Sandhornet Mountain (922 m above sea level). Near Våg is Blixgården where the priest Elias Blix (1836-1902) grew up. A monolith has been erected in commemoration of this multi-faceted man who was a minister of the church, professor of Hebrew, bible translator and - not least - a great hymn writer. His hymns include the song which is often referred to as northern Norway's national anthem 'Å eg veit meg eit land langt der uppe mot nord' [I know of a country far up in the north]. The view across the 50 km long **Salt Fjord**, which is to the south of Bodø, is magnificent. The famous **Saltstraumen** tidal current flows through the 150 m wide strait, which is spanned by a magnificent bridge. Four times a day (between high and low tide), huge quantities of water are forced in or out of the strait - 372 million m³ of water with an average speed of 29 km an hour. The current is strongest when there is a new moon or a full moon and the strait is only negotiable two hours after high and low tide. However, it is possible to fish at any time and is open to anyone. On the southern side of the fjord, Børvasstindan rises 1,180 m above sea level. As we sail towards Bodø, we will pass the runway of one of the country's largest airports which handles a considerable amount of civil and military air traffic. It was of great strategic importance during «The Cold War», used as an intermediary landing strip for U2 spy planes.

Saltstraumen. The sea forces huge quantities of water into the narrow strait at high tide. The water is then forced out again at low tide. This is a paradise for fish (and fishermen).
(Photo: Aune Forlag)

Landegode and Steigen. To the west is the legendary Lofotveggen - a "wall" formed by a chain of islands and sharp peaks rising out of the ocean to the north of Røst. Pause for a moment and think about the thousands of fishermen who left home every winter and sailed to the large seasonal fishing grounds in the Lofot sea to secure vital catches of cod. They came from as far south as Trondheims Fjord, but often did not dare to cross the wide Vest Fjord until they were as far north as Steigen. They gathered here as they waited for decent weather to make the 25-30 km trip over the open fjord in January.

To the east of the route, we will see **Måløy/Skarholmen** lighthouse, the Steigen mountains, historical sites and the trading place of Grøtøy, from where the Lofot fishermen had the shortest journey across Vest Fjord to Henningsvær. The lighthouse on **Landegodeøy Island**, directly west of the route, is a much-photographed subject. With a little luck, you'll capture the 'Landego man', who, according to popular belief, climbs to the highest point of the island, 803 m above sea level.

Landego is one of the more characteristic profiles in northern Norway.
(Photo: TO-FOTO)

Vest Fjord and Ofot Fjord stretch from Skomvær lighthouse and Røst in the south to Narvik in the northeast. This is the route taken by the boats which transport ore to and from Narvik. A railway line runs from Narvik to the large iron ore mines in Kiruna in Sweden. The legendary Moskenes current flows between Værøy Island and Moskenesøy Island and is said to be the world's strongest ocean current. It has been imaginatively described by the American author, Edgar Allan Poe, Jules Verne, and by northern Norway's own poet, Petter Dass!

Lofotveggen: this "wall" measures 100 km in length and rises defiantly from the sea. Atlantic cod are caught on the eastern side which is sheltered by the mountains.

Beyond Moskenes, **Lofotveggen** reveals itself in all its glory. It consists of 100 km of peaks and snow-clad granite and volcanic ravines rising defiantly from the sea. After the Ice Age had shaped the country, mighty Lofotveggen rose out of the Gulf Stream. Huge amounts of cod arrived here every winter to spawn (January-April) and provided the basis for the fishing villages on the islands to the east. In the post-war years, some 20,000 fishermen from the south and north gathered here every year. Now there are only around 3,000 who bring in a catch of around 25,000 tonnes. The Gulf Stream brought with it a mild climate and fish. The catches were hung on huge racks and dried by the wind. With the fish came sea birds. On Røst alone there are normally 450,000 pairs of puffins. Read about Lofoten's bird life in bird life and fishing history under Day 9.

Fishing villages. Today, you can rejoice at the sight of Lofotveggen. Further out to the southwest, a line of fishing villages begins at Stamsund: Ure, Mortsund, Ballstad, Nusfjord, Nesland, Sund, Mølnarodden, Hamnøy, Reine, Moskenes, Sørvågen, Tind and Å. In the course of the evening we stop off at Stamsund and see Henningsvær before arriving at Svolvær late in the evening. But on the return trip south, we travel this distance during the day. (Day 9)

Fishermens' cabins. There are fishermens' cabins everywhere. Lofot fishermen often had to spend the night in the open, sometimes sheltering under their upturned boats. Eventually, simple wooden fishermens' cabins were built. The fishing season was during the winter and demands for a higher standard of accommodation increased, though what was on offer still had to be affordable to the fishermen.

After World War II, the number of fishermen gradually decreased and several fishermen's cabins were left empty and began to deteriorate. However, tourists from all over the world soon discovered this new attraction and arrived in their hundreds. The cabins were restored by their owners and converted into comfortable seaside accommodation. Today, there are hundreds of them ranging from the very simple to hotel standard cabins with toilets and baths. There are restaurants in the close vicinity and fishing trips are also available. Visitors are bound to find something to suit their needs.

The climate can be damp, but the temperature here is the highest in the world in terms of degree of latitude. 68° north is far north of Iceland and the northernmost parts of Canada and Alaska. Svolvær's median temperature is +1.8° C in January/February. For information on Stamsund, see Day 9.

The fishermen's cabins provided fishermen with a simple home during the fishing season. Today, they have been taken over by tourists and provide a comfortable place to stay for those who do not prefer life at sea. (Photo: Samfoto, Steinar Haugberg jr.)

49

N
W E
S

Lopphavet

NORDVESTBANKEN

Fugløykalven Fyr

Torsvåg Fyr   Fugløya

Brynilen

Årviksand

Arnøy

Fugløysundet   Laukøya

Vanna   Kværangs

Sør-Fugløy   **Skjervøy**

Vannsundet

Karlsøy   Kågen

Hansnes   Lyngstuva

MALANGSGRUNNEN

Ringvassøy   Reinøy

Gjøtsundet   Sørkjosen   Storslett
Nordr

Ullsfjord   Lyngen

Lenangstindane   E6
1596

Kaldfjord   **Tromsø**   Olderdalen

Kvaløya   Tromsdalstind   Lyngseidet

Hekkingen   Sommarøy   1238

Ryøya   Fagernes

Husøy   Botnhamn   Jiehkkevarri   Furuflaten
1833

Senjahopen   Rystraumen   Malangen   Balsfjorden

Skaland   Breitinden   Skibotn   Raisdu
985

SVENSGRUNNEN   Gryllefjord   Gibostad   Lenvik Kirke   Senja

Hvalsafari   Horsken   Sifjord   Silsand   Storsteinnes

Andenes   Finnsnes   E6   Nordkjosbotn   Helligskoge
iksøya   Andøya Flyatsjøn   Finnfjordbotn

Bleik   Ånderdalen   Vangsvik   Sørreisa
ela   Nasjonalpark   Målselv

Ramså   Senja   Tranøy Kirke   Bardufoss   Skjold
øya   Dverberg   Stonglandseidet   Dyrøy   Rørstadbotn   Åandselv

Helløya   Andfjorden   Tranøyfjorden

Åse   Bjarkøy   Vågsfjorden

Risøyhamn   Grøtavær   Sandsøya   Selangen   Sjøvegan
Elgsnes   Grytøya   Setermoen

Toppsundet   Andørja   Bardu
Kvæfjord   Lavangen
Rolla   Ibestad

Kvæfjord   Trondenes Kirke   Øvre Dividal
Harstad   Nasjonalpark

Kilbotn   Grovfjord   Gratangen

Flesnes   Revsnes   Kaldsundet   E6
erfjord

H i n n ø y a   Evenskjer   Bjerkvik

Kongsvik   Bogen
salen   Fjeldal

Ramsund   Liland

Evenes   **Narvik**

Lødingen   Ofotfjorden   Beisfjord

Ofotfjorden   Ballangen   E6

Bjørkåsen

HARSTAD

Spend the morning exploring this interesting town.

Facts: 23,000 inhabitants. The local newspaper has over 15,000 subscribers. It has a sheltered location and good harbour. Terraced buildings lead up from the harbour, against a backdrop of forests and mountains. Harstad is a central meeting point for the islands which cluster around Norway's largest island, Hinnøy, which has agricultural areas to the west. Harstad flourished during the 'herring years' at the end of the 1800s and acquired town status in 1904. When herring stocks were exhausted, the town developed industries such as shipbuilding and maintenance, the production of equipment for the shipping industry and the fishing fleets and import of coal from Svalbard. Most recently, the town became the headquarters for oil exploration in the region. Whilst the sea on one side has brought activity to the town, the relatively fertile farming communities to the west and to the north have provided a good basis for the dairy and meat processing industries, which produce land-based products as a supplement to fish products.

Since 1992, northern Norway's cultural festival has been held in Harstad's magnificent cultural centre. Visit the area in the schooner Anna Rogde.
(Photo: TO-FOTO)

The town was once the headquarters for the Norwegian Army's 6th Division and has an officer training school as well as a number of schools of higher education. Oil companies have arrived and have set up relatively modest offices, and the town eagerly awaits the extraction of oil and gas from the Continental shelf to the north.

Northern Norway's cultural festival means that the area has an active cultural life. The annual festival week and the magnificent cultural centre attract diverse cultural activities to the region.

Trondenes, near to the town, and the island of Bjarkøy, slightly to the north, are known in Norway as being the homes of the legendary Asbjørn Selsbane and Tore Hund respectively. Germany's occupying forces built a large coastal fort here as well as the 'Adolf Gun' with its 42 cm shells (the world's largest calibre). The fort was intended to command the approach to Narvik and Tromsø.

The southbound Coastal Express usually arrives at Harstad as the northbound ship leaves the quay.

Places to visit in Harstad:

1. **Trondenes Church and Trondenes historical centre** dating from around 1250 with archaeological findings and the remains of two fortification towers. Memorial to 800 Soviet prisoners of war, 3 km from the town centre. **Trondenes** was a former court. The area's first church was erected by King Eystein in the 1100s, and was probably originally built of wood. When the current stone church was built, it was probably the most important Roman Catholic church in northern Norway.

Town map of Harstad

2. **The Adolf Gun** on the hill above the church has been well preserved and there is a small exhibition in the bunker.

3. **Harstad church** (1958) - a magnificent modern construction boasting unique architecture, stained-glass windows and a beautiful alter piece. Outside the church, there is a statue of Harstad's favourite son, **Hans Egede** (1686-1758) who is often referred to as the Greenland apostle. Intending to be a missionary to the forgotten Norwegians, he travelled to Greenland only to discover that the Norwegians had disappeared (to America?). Instead he became a missionary to the Eskimos. This is also the birthplace of **Olav Engelbrektson** - Norway's last Catholic bishop. (See **Bud**, Day 2).

The first church in Trondenes was probably built of wood. Legend has it that the first Christians in northern Norway were christened in a small lake by the church in 999. Today, the stone church is built on the site of the former court and the seat of the chieftain. (Photo: TO-FOTO)

Near Kvæ Fjord in the west, the farming districts have 3,200 inhabitants. Strawberries are harvested in some of the world's northernmost strawberry fields. Berries are often harvested in August, when people living further south can no longer get hold of such delicacies. The district has a horticultural college (the world's northernmost) which carries out experiments into the cultivation of flowers, berries, bushes and vegetables. There is no lack of ancient relics including monoliths, burial mounds and Sami places of sacrifice.

As we leave Harstad, we have a spectacular view of this fjord area which is rich in history. First we pass Trondenes, where Bishop Jon Sigurd probably carried out the first christenings of children in northern Norway in 999. Just to the north, you can almost see right into the mouth of the Adolf Gun. Next we head north across Vågs Fjord, passing the islands of Grytøy, Sandsøy and Bjarkøy to the west. This is an equally historical trip.

Bjarkøy is the seat of the Bjarkøy family, ancient chieftains of the region, renowned from Snorre's sagas. As the island was strategically situated on the north-south trade route, it wasn't just Norwegians who travelled in the area. History tells of ancient links with the peoples of Northern Russia. Ottar visited them in the 9th century and brought back stories of a well-developed and fertile country at the mouth of several large rivers, where the people spoke a language similar to Sami. Leather goods and products from the Orient were available here. This trade interested the chieftain of Bjarkøy, but there were greater profits to be made from sacking raids and, according to legend, the Norwegians made many of these. Tore Hund was a great merchant who acquired many riches from trade with the Finns and with Russia. In 1026, he pillaged Russian burial grounds and gold treasures. This animosity was probably due to the rivalry over the collection of taxes amongst the Samis, who paid their taxes in pelts. The last Norwegian 'Viking expedition' to Russia was in 1222. From then on, Russians began to retaliate in northern Norway. By then Tore Hund had been dead for 200 years.

Tore was originally one of the king, St. Olav's men, though he was related to Asbjørn Selsbane in Trondenes and Erling Skjalgsson from Sola, who were killed by the king's men. Consequently, Tore Hund joined the men of the North who killed King Olav in the battle of Stiklestad in 1030. Tore was one of the assassins, but was probably troubled by his conscience and disappeared during a pilgrimage to the Holy Land.

The Bjarkøy family continued to produce great men such as Baron Bjarne Ellingson (died in 1313) who served as a guardian to Eirik Magnusson and who was known for being a leader of important diplomatic missions. Erling Vidkunsson was the regent between 1323-1332. The 500-year old Bjarkøy Pot, discovered in an excavation, is a well-known local artefact. Bjarkøy's law is also well known and formed the basis for Magnus Lagabøter's laws. Eiderdown, used in cushions and duvets, was another natural source of wealth. The eider duck was a protected species. Bjarkøy, with its 600 inhabitants, has a Viking club which welcomes its new members by letting them meet Tore Hund in person!

For information on whale safaris in the western seas, see Day 9 Andenes.

To the east is the island of **Dyrøy** which is now linked to the mainland by a bridge. To the west is Norway's second largest island, Senja, boasting a large number of historical sites, the site of Tranøy church (1773) and Anderdalen National Park with its large pine trees and varied countryside. The countryside is different on the coast of Senja which faces the ocean with steep mountains plunging into the sea, and vibrant fishing communities. Senja is now crisscrossed by roads.

Finnfjordbotn on the mainland is a direct contrast to Senja. The factory chimneys of Finnfjordbotn Smelting Works are visible from the boat. The works produces around 50,000 tonnes of ferrosilicon and is powered by cheap hydro-electric power, of which Norway has an ample supply.

The town of **Finnsnes** lies on the straits. You cannot avoid noticing the magnificent Gisund Bridge which links the mainland to Senja, a miniature Norway. It was built in 1972 and is 1,220 m long. The side of Senja closest to the mainland is sheltered and verdant. Fishing provides the basis for life on the outer coast.

Troms Innland with its agricultural regions is to be found further inland. Over the years, thousands of Norwegian soldiers have been stationed at the military camps here in order to defend Norway against attacks from the north and east.

FINNSNES (5,000 inhabitants). The municipality has 11,000 inhabitants. The town is one of the district's most important trading centres, and also has a fishing equipment factory, shipyards, a dairy, banana ripening facilities and other industry. The local newspaper has 7,400 subscribers. Why not stop off in Finnsnes for some shopping?

Heading north, we pass the former trading post of Gibostad and its 400 inhabitants to the west and Lenvik church to the east. We then sail into Malang Fjord which probably marked Norway's northern boundary 1,000 years ago.

The magnificent Gisund Bridge links Norway's second largest island, Senja, to the mainland. The ocean coast of the island is wild, the sea is rich in fish and the coast that faces the mainland is sheltered and more densely populated. (Photo: Helene Winsents)

Ottar from Malangen?

We heard the story of Ottar's 9th century expedition to Northern Russia in the description of Bjarkøy. The same Ottar recounted his story to King Alfred in London, and you can read the tale in King Alfred's handwritten account in the British Museum. In this, Ottar boasts that he lives further north than any other Norseman and that he is a chieftain in Hålogaland (northern Norway). Historians presume that he lived in this district. We know that Lenvik was the country's northernmost church until Håkon Håkonson's time, when the northern boundary was moved to Tromsø church. Archaeologists have not yet discovered Ottar's house, although several 1,000 year-old dwellings have been unearthed. It is possible that he exaggerated his tale (as has always been the Norwegian way). But it is not improbable that he spoke the truth about his 20 cows, 20 sheep, 20 pigs and 600 reindeer.

The route becomes narrower as we approach the island of Kvaløy to the north. The area is covered with historical sites such as the remains of dwellings and burial mounds. Rock carvings found further north are between 2,500 - 4,000 years old. Reaching Rystraumen, we sail through the fastest tidal current on the whole trip. It flows at up to 6 knots per hour. This means excellent catches for the many sports fishermen who visit the area. On the mainland, the mountains around Bals Fjord rise 1,200 m above sea level.

On the island, Ryøy, close to our route, you'll see the unusual sight of 15 musk oxen which come from a herd transported to Norway from Greenland in 1969. New calves are born every year. The animals thrive up here in the north, an area which was once their natural habitat. Do not go ashore here during the mating season! The musk oxen weigh 450 kg and may regard you as a competitor.

The captain will now begin his preparations for arrival at Tromsø, the capital of arctic Norway. West of the southern tip of Tromsøy Island (Håkøybotn) lies the place where, on 22 November 1944, British bombers finally succeeded in sinking the 44,000 tonnes German warship Tirpitz, killing 1,200 men. The wreckage was removed after the war.

TROMSØ

The capital of arctic Norway and the gateway to the Arctic Ocean. Known as the 'Paris of the North', the town currently has 59,000 inhabitants and the municipality covers 2,558 km². 42,000 people subscribe to the two local newspapers.

Tromsøy, the site of the first settlement, is linked to the mainland by a bridge measuring 1,016 m, but the volume of traffic is now so great that a road tunnel has been built under the strait. A tunnel passing under the town itself leads out to the airport (500,000 - 600,000 passengers per year). Further to the west, and among a myriad of islands, is the 1,235 m long bridge to the island of Kvaløy and a tunnel to Ringvassøy Island. When boats were the only means of communication, this was a natural centre. Today, it remains a major junction for land and air traffic.

The first church was built in 1252. The pope called it 'the church close to the heathens'. Tromsø acquired town status in 1794, after Bergen and Trondheim had lost their trade monopoly in northern Norway. Released from the restrictive trade rules imposed by these 'southerners', Tromsø has flourished for the past 200 years. At the same time, Tromsø has developed its own institutions in step with the general development of society. The university is the icing on the cake.

Tromsø is the capital of arctic Norway. It is strategically situated on shipping routes and is a stage for nature's theatre.
(Photo: Nancy Bundt)

For countless generations, sea traffic to and from Northern Russia has been considerable. The hunting of whales, seals and walrus near Spitsbergen gave rise to new traffic with Russian, British, Dutch and German ships visiting the town. The first whaler sailed northwards in 1820. Seal hunting in the Arctic Ocean gradually developed into an extensive industry (without causing stocks to be exhausted). A number of large arctic expeditions led by such men as Nansen, Amundsen and Andrée set out from here. In 1928, Roald Amundsen left Tromsø in the seaplane 'Latham' to rescue his Italian colleague (and competitor) Umberto Nobile. Nobile returned, but Roald Amundsen did not. A statue in his memory has been erected at the harbour.

Town map of Tromsø

The town has been relatively untouched by war. During the Napoleonic Wars (1812) there was a minor confrontation between marine vessels, and in 1944 the German warship, Tirpitz, was sunk here.

The town can boast that it was once Norway's capital. This was in May 1940, when the King and the Norwegian government fled from the south where the Norwegian resistance was beginning to crumble. On 7 June, they were forced to escape to England and continue the fighting from there. Although the Germans had been defeated in Narvik, the Allies gave priority to fronts in continental Europe and abandoned the campaign in Norway. Although **modern Tromsø** is still a seafaring town with industries closely linked to the sea, it is now also a trade and service centre for Troms, with the county's administrative offices located here. The hospital offers a "telemedicine" service that provides medical services wherever you are. The educational sector has a full register of services. The town has 17 schools and colleges with 13,000 students. The university (from 1972) has 4,000 students. Specialities are Saami subjects and fisheries.

Marine biology research is aimed at developing marine farming, the fisheries, agriculture and the biotech industries.

The airport handles over 1/2 million passengers every year. Restaurants are busy both day and night. The world's northernmost brewery has a bar which is open to visitors. (A speciality is Mackøl beer served with gulls' eggs). Shopping in Tromsø is excellent.

Places to visit in Tromsø
1. **Polaria** - an adventure centre with the Arctic, Antarctic and Barents Sea as themes.
2. **Tromsø museum** 4 km from the centre of town, exhibits on north Norwegian archaeology, flora, fauna, boats, historical sites and more recent cultural history (20,000 exhibits). Take special note of the special Sami section which has over 2,000 artefacts.
3. **Nordlysplanetariet [The Northern Lights Planetarium]** is unique. Temporarily closed (2002)
4. **Tromsdalen church**, the Arctic cathedral symbolises the dark period and the northern lights. Europe's largest glass mosaic (140 m²).
5. **Fjellheisen.** Take this cable car to 420 m above sea level for panoramic view of the area. Operates throughout the night when the Midnight Sun is shining.
6. **Tromsø bymuseum [Tromsø museum],** and Polar museum, a number of listed houses and mansions.
7. **Tromsø kunstforening [Tromsø Art Gallery].**
   Don't forget to be back at the Coastal Express in good time!

North of Tromsø and to the west, the route is sheltered by the large islands of Ringvassøy, Reinøy, Vanna and Arnøy. To the east, the country develops into one of Norway's most impressive mountain ranges - the so-called Lyng Alps.

On our journey, we pass secluded Karls Island to the west, a natural base for former settlements. The administrative centre and the church were situated on the island, easily accessible by boat from any direction.

Directly to the south of Karlsøy Island, you'll catch a glimpse of the mountain world of Ulls Fjord. Beware of Lyngstuva, a mountain protruding 390 m from the sea between Ulls Fjord and Lyngen Fjord. Looking east, we see the southern edge of the mysterious Lyng Alps. They are formed from the same type of stone as the Jotunheimen range and consist of countless sharp peaks, often rising 1,300 and 1,500 m above sea level. The highest, Jiekkevarre, is 1,833 m above sea level and is situated far to the south. To the north, Store Jegervasstind (1,596 m above sea level) is the most daunting. This mountain is a veritable climbers' paradise. Although an Englishman, William C. Slingsby, conquered it in 1898, climbers still find it exhilarating to discover new routes.

Lyngen also evokes tragic memories of the winter of 1944/45. The German Army on the

Arctic Ocean front (Kirkenes/Petsamo - to Salla in northern Finland) were on the retreat. Hitler gave the Commander-in-Chief, the Austrian General Lothar Rendulic, orders to destroy all of northern Norway as far south as Lyngen Fjord. At that time, there was no route along the fjord creating a natural defence towards the east. Study the map and you will see why. Consequently, almost every house between Lyngen and the border to the east of Kirkenes was burnt, and the people were forcibly evacuated. There's scarcely an old house to be seen until you begin your return journey.

Fugløy Island, to the north, is home to 200,000 pairs protected puffins and lies at the mouth of the fjord.
We are now making our way towards Nord-Troms' largest fishing village, Skjervøy, although we don't stop here until our return journey, see Day 8.

Lyngen Fjord cuts through a rugged landscape of soaring mountains -
a mountain climbers' paradise for more than 100 years.
(Photo: Samfoto, Ragnar Flislid)

THE NORTHERN LIGHTS - AURORA BOREALIS - AND WIND POWER ......

The Northern Lights are a natural phenomenon which occurs in arctic regions in particular. The phenomenon is caused by electrically-charged solar particles, high in energy, entering the earth's atmosphere. This usually occurs in an area around the Arctic Circle (67° N). Within this area, the Northern Lights may be seen almost every night, but are seen less and less as you travel south. The phenomena are not visible when it is cloudy.

The colours are particularly beautiful during the winter nights. The lights are usually yellow-green, but can also be green or reddish-violet. The magnificent colours light up the sky and usually form a bow from east to west or a slightly more even belt of colour. The formations can arise at any moment, filling the sky at an incredible speed. The lowest point of the Northern Lights is usually around 100 km above the ground. Størmer and Birkeland are Norway's greatest researchers into the Northern Lights. The Northern Lights Observatory in Tromsø was built in 1928 with money from the Rockefeller Foundation and Tromsø Museum houses a modern Northern Lights exhibition.

Wind power. Windmills.
In 2001 there were only 23 windmills in Norway – some of them at Vikna. We are now getting two giant "Wind Power Parks" at Smøla and west of Tromsø, and possibly three medium size parks at Stadtlandet, Hitra and near Havøysund (Finnmark). Opponents believe that the windmills spoil the coastal landscape and the power generated will be too expensive, but the editor believes that development will be rapid, with improved technology and increasing acceptance of this new element in the landscape.

N
W E
S

NORDKAPPBANKEN

AUSTHAVET

Kinnarodden
Bispen
Sletnes Fyr
Gamvik
Mehamn Lufthavn
Mehamn
Oksfjorden
Smørbringa
Omgangsstauran

Knivskjellodden
Nordkapp
Gjesværstappan
Skarsvåg
Helnes Fyr
NORDKYN-
HALVØYA
Tanahorn
Berlev
Berlevåg L

Hjelmsøystauren
Gjesvær
Kamøyfjorden
Finnekjerka
Kjøllefjord

Fruholmen Fyr
Hjelmsøy
Magerøya
Valan
Nordvågen
Tufjorden

Ingøy
Masøy
Honningsvåg
Sværholtklubben
Hopseidet

Havøysund
Kåfjord
Tanafjorden

Rolvsøy
Magerøysundet
Ishavsveien

Bakfjorden
Kolbvfjorden
Repvåg

Rolvsøysundet

Revsbotn
Lebesby
Rustefjelbma

Hammerfest
Ifjord
VA
Rypefjord
Kokelv
Ifjordfjellet

Kvaløya

Kvalsund
Olderfjord
Tana bru
Vestr
Skaidi
Skipagurra

Seiland
iilandsjøkulen
*981
E6
E6
Børselvfjellet
FINNMARKSVIDDA
E6
Polmak

Sennalandet

Stabbursdalen
Nasjonalpark
Rasttigaisa
*1067
Utsjoki

Lakselv
Banak
Levajok
Tanaelva

Cohkarassa
*1139

alvik

*Alta
FINNLAND

E6
E6

Sautso Kraftstasjon
Jiesjavrre
Tanaelva

Suolavuopmi

Maze/Masi
Karåsjok

Today, you can spend the morning relaxing as there will be plenty of time to enjoy Hammerfest and Havøysund on our return journey, on Day 8. The captain is eager to move on to Honningsvåg to show you what millions of people only dream of seeing: Europe's northernmost outpost, the North Cape.

However, if you are interested in reading about Hammerfest and Havøysund, turn to Day 8.

We will now be concentrating on what lies ahead: Magerøy Island and the North Cape.

Måsøy Island, to the north of our route, has been the site of a church since 1746, some 250 years ago. There have always been rich fishing grounds nearby, and the island has always been an active fishing community. However, it is not only people who settle close to rich stocks of fish: Magerøy Island, northeast of Gjesvær, is home to a myriad of bird species. There are an amazing 400,000 pairs of puffins living in the Stappan/Gjesværstappan colony spread over three small islands.

Måsøy has played host to many grand visitors. In 1795, Louis Philippe (1773-1850), crown prince of France, visited Måsøy en route to the North Cape. He stayed with a merchant called Buch for the duration of his stay. His trip around Europe was an attempt to avoid assassins as, during this time, the heads of French royalty were not safe! Louis Philippe was later declared king and reigned until the February Revolution of 1848. In 1838, he sent a frigate, Recherche, to northern Norway to deliver a statue. This statue was twice life size and was given in thanks for the hospitality he was shown during his exile. The statue remained in Havøysund (the administrative centre) until it was destroyed, together with the entire settlement, by General Rendulic's troops in 1944. Today, a replica can be seen at the North Cape. Måsøy is also the birthplace of M.B. Landstad, a great hymn writer (1802).

Life on the Coastal Express does not only consist of sightseeing, there is also a relaxed holiday atmosphere on board. But don't waste your time sleeping. As a well-known north Norwegian proverb goes: 'You'll have time to sleep when you get to the south'.
(Photo: Helene Winsents)

The Coastal Express enters Magerøysundet Strait, between Magerøy and the mainland. This is a busy shipping lane used by trawlers, cargo vessels and cruise ships travelling to and from Russia and the Barents Sea. In 1993 archaeologists found the remains of dwellings here that are 10,300 years old – several thousand years older than the Egyptian pyramids
.**HONNINGSVÅG**, with its 2,800 inhabitants, is the capital of the North Cape. The municipality has 3,500 inhabitants. A car ferry used to be the link with the mainland (Kåfjord) but a new road opened in the summer of 1999 with a 6.8 km undersea tunnel replacing the ferry.
In the spring, the Norwegian Army's landing craft transport around 3,800 reindeer over Magerøy Strait to their summer pastures on Magerøy Island. However, during the autumn, when it is time for the reindeer to return to the snow-clad plains of Karasjok, the animals and their calves, born at the end of May/beginning of June, swim across the 1,800 m wide strait.
The excellent harbour at Honningsvåg eventually developed into a large fishing port, which in turn led to growth in the fishing, processing and refrigeration industries and trade in capelin fish meal and capelin oil. The Norwegian State College of Fisheries is located on the outskirts of Honningsvåg. Between 4,000 and 5,000 ships enter the harbour here every year, bringing trade and industry to the area. Ships also bunker here. Pilots from the local pilot station are vital necessity for boats in the area. The airport handles around 19,000 passengers every year and 1,300 people subscribe to the local newspaper.

Honningsvåg is not just a Coastal Express harbour and the point of departure for trips to the North Cape. It is situated on the main shipping route to Northern Russia and all the riches of the mighty Barents Sea.
(Photo: Nancy Bundt)

Places to visit in Honningsvåg.
1. **The North Cape Museum** has exhibits depicting the history of fishing and tourism at the North Cape.
2. **The North Cape House** houses a tourist information office, a gallery and a souvenir shop.
3. **Honningsvåg Church** (1884) should not be missed. It was the only building left standing after Rendulic razed the town to the ground in 1944.

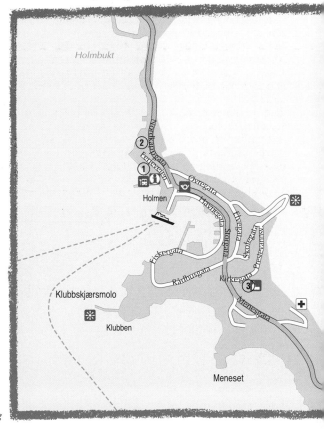

Town map of Honningsvåg

THE NORTH CAPE.
The North Cape Road stretches for 34 km. During the winter, it is open as far as Skarsvåg (21 km away). The last 13 km (to the plateau) are open between 1 May and mid-October. During the winter, you can rent full winter gear and visit the place by snow-mobile or sleigh. Weather permitting, it is possible to drive to Skipsfjord Mountain (15 km from Honningsvåg) from where you can see the North Cape. You will only have time for this if you stay here more than one day.

On our journey to the North Cape we cross the 71st parallel, an airport, a camp site, a youth hostel and (during the summer) Sami camps. Drivers must be careful not to run over the many reindeer grazing on the island. From Skipsfjord Mountain (15 km from Honningsvåg), you will catch your first glimpse of the North Cape Plateau, with Hornet to the north. Duken Mountain is instantly recognisable by its whiteness. A number of species of flowers, otherwise only seen in Siberia and on Svalbard, grow here. It is possible that some of them survived the last Ice Age.

Skarsvåg is Norway's northernmost fishing village. Main features include its fishing industry, swimming pool and the flowers in its gardens. To the west, is the site of a former fishing village dating back to the late Middle Ages. This was also the site of a whaling station in the last half of the 19th century.

For more than 100 years, people from all over the world have dreamt of visiting Europe's northernmost point. It is a noble monument, unsurpassed by any other, and will probably still be here thousands of years from now.

The North Cape

Next we cross the North Cape plateau which rises 307 m above the sea. In the past (before the road was built) tourists climbed the 1,008 steps from Hornvika. You are now 71° 10' 21" north of the Equator, 2,080 km from the North Pole. Europe's northernmost point is the small headland, Knivskjellodden, to the west of the plateau, (71° 11' 8"). A marked footpath leads to this point.

The North Cape in years gone by

The North Cape was given its name by Richard Chancellor, a British seafarer who, in 1553, was searching north of Siberia for the Northeast Passage to India. This led to a considerable amount of British trade with Murmansk/Archangel, and for the next 30 years there was uncertainty as to who had the sovereign rights to the area. Over the years, many famous people have visited the area. These include Louis Philippe of Orleans in 1795 who was grateful for the hospitality shown to him during his exile from France. When he finally became king, he sent the town a statue which stood here until 1944. Read about this under the entry for Måsøy. The present statue is a replica of the original and was donated by the French government. In 1873, the Swedish/Norwegian king, Oscar II visited. He walked from Hornvika to unveil a commemorative stone. In his speech he declared that 'This proud rock is the final gem in the silver tiara which crowns 'The Scandinavian Peninsula''. On 25 December 1943, a sea battle took place off the North Cape, during which the German warship, "Scharnhorst", was sunk. Of the 1,934 men on board the ship, only 36 were rescued. In 1973, Tina Zuccoli, an Italian botanist and teacher, published a book called 'Flora Arctica', and raised money amongst school children in Modena for a statue of the Madonna and Child. Simon Flem Devold, a Norwegian author of children's books, was the driving force behind the monument 'Children of the World' which can be seen here and which exhibits themes contributed by children from 7 different countries.

The North Cape Hall has been built into the rock and offers a panoramic view, a superb exhibition accompanied by wide screen video films, souvenir shops, a post office and much more. Why not become a member of the Royal North Cape Club here? There is also an ecumenical chapel here which can be used for meditation and prayer. You could even arrange to get married here, celebrating with champagne.

At the edge of the world

In 1664, an Italian called Negri, wrote 'I am standing at the edge of the world here at the North Cape at Finnmark's outermost point. This is where the world ends, and this is also where my curiosity ends, and I can return home satisfied'. We, however, continue east on the Coastal Express.

The wide and imposing **Porsanger Fjord** is 120 km long and 19 km wide at its mouth. **Sværholtklubben** is one of the world's large bird colonies. It is not unusual to see a sea eagle circling above its victims. In the past, 10,000 eggs were gathered here and protected. **Lakse Fjord**, 80 km long and 22 km wide, forms the border with the large Nordkinn/Nordkyn peninsula. The approach to **Kjølle Fjord** is magnificent and Finnkjerka, Norway's most elegant cliff formation, not conquered until 1955, soon comes into sight. In the fjord near Oksvåg is the world's northernmost birch forest. Kjølle Fjord is of course a <u>fishing village</u> and the centre for Lebesby municipality with its 1,400 inhabitants. Though there are agricultural areas around the fjord, there are vast regions here which remain uninhabited. The church was a present from Denmark after the war. **Nordkyn** (Nordkinn) is a large peninsula which appears to be carved out of the sea. Although it does not protrude as far north as North Cape, Kinnarodden is mainland Europe's northernmost point 71° 8' 0" N , in other words approximately 2' further south than the North Cape. We sail north of this peninsula, passing the bird colony at Smørbringa on our way.

Nothing can compare with nature's own architecture. No cathedral is more magnificent than Finnkjerka. (Photo: TO-FOTO)

MEHAMN

Next we pass Kinnarodden. Further up the fjord is the fishing village of **Mehamn**. The airport handles around 14,000 passengers annually. Mehamn Hotel has mainland Europe's northernmost hotel room (no. 301). The hotel in Longyearbyen on Svalbard is of course far further north. Further to the east is **Bispen Mountain** (in the shape of a bishop at his pulpit). Yet further to the east is mainland Europe's northernmost lighthouse, Sletnes. Fruholmen lighthouse to the northwest of Havøysund lies further north, but is on an island.

Next we pass by Gamvik, which used to correspond with the Coastal Express by small boats, which was quite normal at many of the ports, virtually always without accident. Fish and fresh air are also important aspects of life in Gamvik. The municipality has 1,200 inhabitants (including Mehamn), a guesthouse, church and a cultural historical exhibition. Catch up on your sleep as we cross Austhavet.

Eastern Finnmark awaits us. Norway's much bigger than you thought, isn't it!

THE SAMI......

The Sami inhabit a large area which lies to the north of the Kola peninsula in Russia, crossing Finnish and Swedish Lappland as far as Northern Norway and including the inland areas of central Norway as far south as Femunden, south of Røros. There are far more Sami in Norway than in Sweden and Finland: estimates suggest between 30,000 and 60,000 Sami live in Norway - taking into account the degree of intermarriage with Norwegians and Finns. (Finnish-speaking Norwegians)

The majority of Sami in Norway live and work like most Norwegians. Statistically, only 10 % of Sami (statistics show 2,800 reindeer farming Saami, of which 2,100 in Finnmark.) keep reindeer for a living. They own 148,000 reindeer, of which 103,000 can be found in Finnmark. During the winter, the reindeer live off moss which they find under the snow on the mountain plains. They are constantly guarded by their owners. In the summer, they also graze in coastal areas and on some of the islands where the owners have set up camp, (eg. around the North Cape).

The Sami are made up of three language groups: the northern Sami live in Finnmark, Troms and part of Nordland. A small group called the Lule Sami live south of Narvik, particularly in the area around Tys Fjord. The southern Sami live further south, for the most part in the areas bordering Sweden - from Saltfjellet (the Arctic Circle) in the north, to Femunden south of Rorøs. They have their own language, into which a portion of the Bible was recently translated.

The Sami language has the same standing as Norwegian, and several municipalities in Finnmark have Sami names. A Sami Parliament is elected by all Sami people registered in Norway. The first parliament was opened by King Olav in the Sami capital of Karasjok.

N
W E
S

NKEN

AUSTHAVET

Finnmark Øst
(Gass- og oljeboring)

BARENTSHAVET

Kinnarodden
Bispen
Sletnes Fyr
Gamvik
Mehamn Lufthavn
Oksfjorden
Mehamn
Smørbringa
Omgangsstauran

kapp

Helnes Fyr
øyfjorden
Valan
Nordvågen
Honningvåg
ndet
fjord
epvåg
fjorden

Finnekjerka
Kjøllefjord
Sværholtklubben

NORDKYN-
HALVØYA

Tanahorn
Berlevåg
Berlevåg Lufthavn
Kongsøyfjorden
Makkaur Fyr

Hopseidet

Laksefjorden

Tanafjorden

Kongsfjord
Båtsfjord
Båtsfjord Flyplass
Syltefjorden

Syltefjordsstauran
Hamningberg

Persfjorden

Hornøya
Vardø Fyr
Vardø
Vardø Lufthavn
Domen
Kiberg

Lebesby

Ishavsveien

VARANGERHALVØYA

Komagvær

Ifjord
Ifjordfjellet

Rustefjelbma

Skallelv

Børselvfjellet

Tana bru
Skipagurra

Vestre Jakobsel
Vadsø
St. Ekkerøy

Varangerfjorden

E6
Polmak

E6

Bugøynes
Ranvika

Bøkfjord Fyr
Bøkfjorden
Jarfjorden
Grense Jakobselv

FINNMARKSVIDDA

Rasttigaisa
* 1067
Levajok
Utsjoki

Kirkenes Lufthavn
Kirkenes
Storskog
Neiden
Bjørnevatn
Boris Gleb
(Russland)
E6

Tanaelva

Sør-Varanger

Svanvik
* 96
Nikel

E6
E6

Tanaelva

FINNLAND

Pasvikelva

Karåsjok

RUSSLAND

Øvre Pasvik
Nasjonalpark

VADSØ has a population of 6,100 and is the local administrative centre. Around 70,000 passengers pass through the airport annually, and the local paper has 7,600 subscribers. The original site of the town was on the island of Vadsø itself, but it later moved to a more sheltered site on the mainland. It became a local trade centre in 1833. During the 19th century, there was a strong influx of Finns who, fleeing the famine in their homeland, came here to take advantage of the rich supply of fish. In 1875, two thirds of all inhabitants were Finnish-speaking; persons of Finnish descent. Finnish is taught in schools and still spoken in many districts, including the Vadsø - Vardø coast.

The district's main industries are fishing and public administration. The fishing industry is large, although there are no longer many active fishermen. In February and March, shoals of capelin come in from the ocean to spawn, and the fish oil plants are kept busy. Cod follow the capelin between March and June, although they rarely come all the way into Varanger Fjord. A new species of giant crab, the Kamptsjatka crab, is now spreading into the fjord from northern Russia.

Vadsø is the administrative centre of Finnmark, and the centre of the Kveni (Finnish) culture. Like everything else in the town, the church had to be rebuilt after the war. (Photo: Knudsens Fotosenter)

What to see in Vadsø.

Vadsø Museum celebrates Finnish immigration, the Finnish language and Finnish culture. Exhibits include remains of fishing implements and two old town buildings which have survived despite the fact that the town was almost completely destroyed during the war.

The immigrant memorial by Finnish sculptor Ensio Seppänen in the town centre. It was unveiled by President Kekkonen, King Carl Gustav and King Olav in 1977.

The mooring mast of the airship "Norge", which was used by Roald Amundsen in 1926 and Umberto Nobile in 1928. It is located to the east of the Coastal Express quay.
Vadsø church (1958). Architect Magnus Poulsson.

What was "pomor" trading? This was a form of barter between Russians and Norwegians which lasted for a considerable length of time. Vadsø was the centre of this trade in the 19th and 20th centuries. The traders spoke a "pidgin" Russian/Norwegian that everyone understood.

Varanger Fjord is 95 km long and 55 km wide at its mouth. Archaeologists have made sensational findings to the north and south and further up the fjord to the west. These suggest that the area was inhabited as early as 9,000 BC and the remains of several hundred homes have been unearthed here. The inner part of the fjord is a Sami heartland, and the municipality has changed its name from Nesseby to Unjarga.

KIRKENES and the surrounding settlements have 5,000 inhabitants. It is the centre of Sørvaranger municipality which has 9,500 inhabitants. The town is sandwiched between two time zones – Helsinki and Moscow – and is in the heart of 'border country'. The town is south of the Arctic timberline and is very fertile compared with the rest of the Finnmark coast.The town is located at the mouth of Pasvikelva river which forms part of the border with

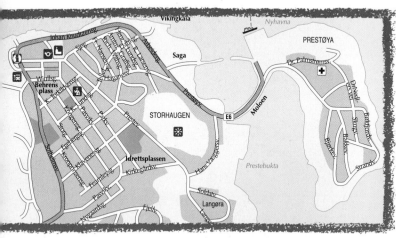

Town map of Kirkenes

Russia. The E6 road ends here and it is also the terminus for Norwegian flights.
The airport handles 155,000 passengers annually, and there are around 120,000 border crossings annually at Storskog on the border with Russia. As the harbour is far up the fjord, the Gulf Stream does not reach it and it freezes often. Ice-breakers are often used to open up the harbour. Kirkenes was built up around the mining company AS Sydvaranger, but the mining operations have now closed down and the most important industries are trade with Russia, ship repairs, tourism and the service sector. Local newspaper with a circulation of 4,000.

What to do in Kirkenes

Bus and taxi services to the town centre coincide with the arrival and departure times of the Coastal Express. If your stay is long enough you can visit:

Grenselandmuseet [Border Museum] – with exhibitions linked to the border area shared by Norway, Finland and Russia.

River boat safari – a historical trip through the estuary of Pasvikelva river to the border at Boris Gleb.

Andersgrotta – bomb shelter from World War II. A 10-minute video is shown on the war in the north. Norwegian, English and German text.

Saviomuseet – an art museum displaying works from the Sami artist John Savio (1902-1938).

Prestfjellet – residential area with stunning view over the town and fjord.

Russian border at Storskog (15 km) – the official border crossing to Russia. From Elvenes there is a view of Boris Gleb, the small Russian power station community, where there is a red 'Skolte Sami' chapel.

The mines at Bjornevatn (11 km) – large open-cast mine which is a monument to over 90 years of mining history. The mines also contain the tunnel in which 2,500 people sought shelter for 2 months in the autumn of 1944 before the Russians liberated the area on 26 October. Ten children were born in the tunnel.

*Leaving Kirkenes, you've only seen half of what the coast has to offer. Prepare yourself for many new experiences.
(Photo: TO-FOTO)*

Pasvikdalen – border valley which stretches south for one kilometre between Russia and Finland. Renowned for its eastern flora and fauna and Norway's most easterly group of bears. You can visit the Strand museum, Bjørnehi, 96-høyda (viewpoint over Pasvikdalen and the Russian mining town of Nikel), Øvre Pasvik Nasjonalpark and Treriksrøysa.

Neiden (40 km) – salmon fishing with casting nets is permitted here in Skoltefossen in July. Old east Sami tradition which is now practised by everybody in the community.

Bugøynes (100 km) – picturesque fishing station which has preserved its Finnish architecture because the town avoided being destroyed during World War II. Finnish is still spoken here today.

Grense-Jakobselv (60 km) – small settlement on the Arctic Ocean. Only a narrow river separates it from Russia and there are excellent views of the Russian watch tower on the other side. The King Oscar II chapel (1869) was a spiritual reminder to the east. Beautiful sandy beach on the Arctic Ocean.

The border with the east was fixed in 1826. Before that, the municipality was a common area between Russia and Norway/Sweden. When Finland became independent in 1919, it was allowed access to the coast via the Petsamo corridor. Finland lost Petsamo afer 1945, at which point Norway gained a border with the Soviet Union. During World War II, the area became the base for the Wehrmacht's offensive against the Soviet Union's ice-free port of Murmansk. The cost was 328 bombing raids by Soviet planes and total destruction before the Nazis finally retreated. During the Cold War, the Iron Curtain was well and truly in place along the border and contact with former neighbours to the east was very limited. Today new relationships are being forged across the border and cross-border traffic is flourishing.

The frontier between east and west - the former Iron Curtain - passed through here. We all hope for a prosperous mutual future from the North Cape to Archangel. (Photo: Knudsens Fotosenter)

The Vadsø - Vardø coastal road.

The settlements along the low-lying coastal strip, which are home to the Finnish-speaking Kveni, are strung together like a string of pearls. Archaeological finds indicate settlements between 900 and 9,000 years old, based around fishing. Ekkerøy Island is home to a bird colony, and the rivers Skallelv and Komagelv provide excellent salmon fishing. Kiberg (pop. 500) still has German World War II fortifications and guns from old German cruisers. **Domen** Mountain (127 m above sea level), closer to Vardø, is where witches met for Midsummer's Eve and Christmas celebrations with the Devil. During the 17th century, 80 witches were burnt here - the last of them as late as the early 1700s.

VARDØ, on Vardøya, is connected to the mainland by a subsea tunnel (2,892 m), and its harbour and airport are located on the mainland (around 13,000 passengers annually). It has a population of 2,700. Fishing and fish processing have naturally been the town's staple industries, and many fishing boats from the town still serve the fish processing plants. The "pomor" trade with the Russians was also important, although this has not been the case since the Russian Revolution. Vardø was, however, of vital importance to NATO's early warning system during the Cold War, but the domes have also had civilian uses. Local newspaper with a circulation of 1,500.

The most easterly point in Norway is the bird colony on Hornøya Island off Vardø.
The town has marked the eastern limit of Norway since 1307. Salute Vardøhus Fort!
(Foto: Helene Winsents)

The expansion of the Russian Empire around 1300 put an end to fur hunting on Kola, and the Russians threatened Varanger. Vardø church, consecrated by Archbishop Jørund in 1307, was intended to mark Norwegian interests. Shortly afterwards, the first fortresses were built by Håkon V as a bulwark against Russian and Karelian raiders. The Sami were often caught between taxpayers from both east and west. The present Vardøhus Fort was built between 1734 and 1738, and has stood fast against invaders from the east. It is the reason that Varanger is still Norwegian territory today. It has never actually been touched by war, and apart from some anti-aircraft fire in 1940, it only fires its guns on one special day every year. This is when the whole sun finally appears above the horizon, usually around 21 January, and Vadsø school children are given a day off. The town became a trading centre in 1789, and 2/3 of the town was destroyed between 1942 and 1944.

Norway's most easterly point is Hornøya Island close to the town. It is located at 31° 10' 10" East, in other words further east than St. Petersburg and Istanbul. (Did you know that parts of Norway are in Eastern Europe?) The island is home to a protected bird colony and is also the site of the 2 million candle-power Vardø Lighthouse which can be seen over 23 nautical miles away.

What to see in Vardø?

Vardøhus Fort, from 1737, is a well-preserved octagonal fort with 4 towers, 10 cannons and a small museum. In the coastguard hut you can see the remains of an earlier fort - Kongestokken - with the signatures of Christian IV, Prince Vladimir, Oscar II, Haakon VII, Olav V and Harald V. The best looked after tree in Norway is an old rowan which is wrapped up by soldiers in October and unpacked again in April. This must be the only fort in the world to have carried out its historic mission for 250 years without ever having to fire a single shot, save for the salute to the returning sun in January.

Vardøhus Museum exhibits collections based on local heritage, natural history and military themes.

Vardø church dating from 1958.

The sun is below the horizon from 23 November to 21 January - 59 days in all. To make up for it, however, it shines non-stop from 16 May to 29 July. Just imagine: 79 days without a sunset!

The Barents Sea is on Vardø's doorstep, and is the site of Russian and Norwegian fishing cooperation on the setting of catch quotas. They disagree, however, as to the "centre line" principle for the border between the two countries' economic zones. At the moment the area of contention is the neutral 'grey zone' which covers an area as large as one third of Norway's considerable land area. They do agree, however, that 'the loophole' - an area outside the economic zones in international waters - must be managed by the two countries as a spawning ground for the Barent cod.

Hamningberg, 40 km from Vardø, is an abandoned fishing village located in a wild and rugged landscape where the wind and waves have been allowed to work the mountains through millennia. The village is now a holiday centre, and can be reached by road during the summer or snowmobile in winter. There are remains of warehouses and houses from the time of the pomor trade between Russia and Norway, when large quantities of dried cod were exported to Russian Catholics. The town is mentioned in 16th century Catholic taxation documents, Kapell (1949).

Syltefjordstauran, with Storalkestauren within view, has a colony of rare gannets on its peak.

Stauran is home to millions of birds, including Norway's largest population of kittiwakes.

BÅTSFJORD occupies a sheltered position in the fjord and has a good harbour. Ishavsveien (the Arctic Road) from the E6 over the mountain is open all year. 15,000 passengers pass annually through the airport, and the municipality has a population of 2,400. The Germans did not raze the town during their retreat in 1944, enabling the Norwegian authorities to use it as a supply base. Båtsfjord is one of the major catch landing centres for the Norwegian fishing industry, and has several fish processing factories, a freezing plant, a filleting factory and ship repair yards. The church dates from 1971. At 241.8 m high, the TV mast is the highest in Norway.

Notice the stripes in the cliffs. The sandstone strata were formed under water and then folded under land movement. The sandstone is home to interesting flora and, believe it or not, remains of Stone Age settlements have also been found here.

BERLEVÅG municipality has a population of 1,200. A road, which is open all year round, leads over the mountain to E6 and the airport handles 9,000 passengers every year. Fish is brought to Berlevåg from the well-stocked fishing grounds. As the harbour is open to the ocean and has no natural protection, the Coastal Express was unable to dock here for many years. It was even more difficult for fishing vessels which could not seek shelter from the storms. On two occasions most of the fleet was destroyed, and on two occasions the great stone mole was crushed by storms. In 1973, a new mole was ready, constructed of tetrapods - four-armed, 15 tonne concrete giant blocks - which are connected in such a way that the water can pass through them. Waves as high as 9.8 m have not yet been able to break the mole. It has broken the force of the waves and granted shelter to the fleet. Berlevåg has several fishing industry plants, a ship-builder, a Church from 1960 and a harbour museum – and not least Berlevåg Mandssangforening [Male Choir].Tanahorn Mountain, which used to be a sacrificial site for the Sami, rises 269 m above sea level to the west of the harbour. But enough - it's bedtime for the writer!

Berlevåg faces the Barents Sea. French engineers were needed to construct the tetrapod mole as a protection against storm waves. (Photo: Ola Røe)

The sun never takes a break here in northern Norway - a land where the light never fails to inspire. The country has always been known as "the Land of the Midnight Sun", but even this cannot convey the enduring beauty to be found here in "the Land of Light and Darkness".

The variations of light associated with the special coastal landscape is the most distinctive feature of the region. In addition to the midnight sun and the dark winters, the period of dusk between light and dark creates a relaxing and calming mood compared with the energising force of the sun. In northern Norway, the dusk often lasts a couple of hours every day during the winter, a season which also sees the heavenly cascades of the Northern Lights. Nothing can equal the sight of moonlight playing across the ocean and the snow-clad mountains.

You cannot experience northern Norway to the full without being captivated by the variations in light and the sheer emotional experience of the "Land of Excitement". This far north, you'll come to understand that the locals yearn for the sun when it hasn't been seen for two long months.

One place to experience the display of light is at Vardøhus Fort. For almost 700 years, the fortification has protected Finnmark and kept the area firmly in the hands of Norway. The only shots ever to be fired by the cannons at the fort, however, are the salutes to the sun on 21 January every year when it appears over the horizon. The table provides information about the sun's annual progression.

	22. March sun rises/sets		22. June sun rises/sets		22. Sept. sun rises/sets		22. Dec. sun rises/sets		Dusk 22. March /Sept.	Dusk 22. Dec.
Bergen:	06.35	18.58	03.14	22.08	06.26	18.36	09.49	15.27	41 min.	56 min.
Trondheim:	06.14	18.40	02.06	22.34	06.06	18.16	10.07	14.28	45 min.	69 min.
Bodø: below the horizon 15. Dec.-30. Dec. Midnight sun 02. June-10. July	05.56	18.26	Midnight sun		05.49	18.01	Dark period		53 min.	122 min.
Tromsø: below the horizon 25. Nov.-16. Jan. Midnight sun 17. May-25. July	05.36	18.10	Midnight sun		05.29	17.43	Dark period		57 min.	125 min.
Hammerfest: below the horizon 20. Nov.-23. Jan. Midnight sun 13. May-31. July	05.16	17.52	Midnight sun		05.10	17.25	Dark period		60 min.	126 min.

N
W E
S

Snøhvit
Albatross
Askeladden

Gjesv
Hjelmsøystauren
Fruholmen Fyr
Hjelmsø
Ingøy
Havøysund
Rolvsøy
Bakfjorden
Rolvsøysundet
Revsbotn

TROMSØFLAKET

Sandøyfjorden

Hammerfest
Rypefjord
Kvaløya

Dønnesfjorden
Slettnes
Sørøya
Sørvær
Kvalsund
Andotten
Breivikbotn
Seiland
Hasvik
Nordmannsjøkulen
1075* Seilandsjøkulen
* 981

Sennalandet
E6

Lopphavet
Stjernøya

Loppa
Silda
Bergsfjord
Øksfjord
Altafjorden
Stab
Nas

Fugløykalven Fyr
Tørsvåg Fyr
Fugløya
Øksfjordjøkelen
1204 *

Årviksand
Brynilen
* Jøkelfjorden
Talvik

Amøy
Laukøya
Langfjordbotn
E6
Kåfjord
Alta
Vanna
Kværangsfjorden
Skjervøy
Fugløysundet

r-Fugløy
Vannsundet
Karlsøy
Kågen
E6
Hansnes
Lyngstuva

Ringvassøy
Reinøy
Sautso Kraftstasjon

Grøtsundet
Sørkjosen
Storslett
Suolavuopmi
Lyngen
Nordreisa

Ullsfjord
Lenangstindane
E6
*
1596

fjord
Tromsø
Olderdalen
Maze/Masi
Tromsdalstind
Lyngseidet
1238
Kvaløya
Fagernes

Raisduottarhaldi
Balsfjorden
Jiehkkevarri
*
1833
Furuflaten

Skibotn
Reisa
Nasjonalpark

ke
Reisaduottarhaldi
*

Størsteinnes
E6 °Nordkjosbotn
Helligskogen
Kautokeino

Målselv
ufoss
Aandsely
Kjold

HAVØYSUND - TROMSØ

Bidding farewell to Finnmark, we spend a fascinating day sailing along its coast. **Honningsvåg and Måsøy** are described under Day 6. The day begins in **HAVØYSUND**, the centre of a huge island kingdom. The majority of the population has moved from the outlying islands to Havøysund. Located near the shipping lanes, this traditional fishing village with its own harbour has a population of 1,400. Before the war, its population was only 150, despite the rich fishing grounds nearby.

Today, we know that there are major gas and oil deposits off the coast. However, any landing will no doubt be established in Hammerfest. Although Havøysund will never become an 'oil metropolis', there will be plenty of fish here for a long time yet, providing the fishing industry with ample raw material.

Although Havøysund now has an all-year road to the E6 highway, the sea route is more natural in this kingdom of fish and birds. (Photo: Jon M. Fjelstad)

All the fishing villages along the coast of Finnmark are now linked to the E6 highway throughout the year. The distance from Havøysund is 82 km. As part of 'Operation Reconciliation', German idealists have built a chapel along the road, at Kokelv, and you will find other churches in Havøysund, Måsøy, Ingøy and Rolvsøy. Fruholmen, Europe's most northerly lighthouse, flashes off the coast of Ingøy. To the north, off the northern coast of Hjelmsøy on Hjelmsøystauren, you will find Europe's largest colony of razorbills and guillemot. This rock is home to around 250,000 birds. The Coastal Express does not sail as far out as this. In the past, ships blew their whistles as they passed the colony causing the birds to take flight in their thousands. Today, however, this is frowned upon. Sailing down the strait of Rolvsøysund, on course for Sørøysund, we round the northern tip of Kvaløya and head in towards Hammerfest.

HAMMERFEST has always been regarded as the world's <u>most northerly town at 70° 39'</u> 48". It lies roughly at the same degree of latitude as the <u>northernmost parts of Siberia,</u> <u>Point Barrow, the northernmost point in Alaska,</u> the islands north of Canada and the <u>centre of Greenland</u>. The effect of the Gulf Stream is apparent here. Hammerfest has always been a fishing port, and was granted market status in 1789 when trading monopolies along the coast were dissolved. Although the town's 40 inhabitants were exempt from taxation, no population explosion occurred. It was not until the end of the Napoleonic Wars that the population exceeded 350. Today, the population numbers 7,000 and the town lies at the heart of a municipality of 9,000. Trapping expeditions to the Northern Arctic Ocean and trade with Russia brought growth to the town, as did the expanding trawler fleet which brought in regular catches for the developing fish processing industry.

Not many people know that Britain's mainland blockade against Napoleon stretched this far north. Finnmark purchased grain from Russia, and the British wanted to fill this 'hole' in the isolation of Norway and Denmark. In 1809, the brigs 'Snake' and 'Fancy' shelled the town. At Fuglenes you can still see the earthworks which are all that remains of the fortifications. They were equipped with two small cannons with which the brave citizens of the town defended themselves.

For almost 200 years, Hammerfest has been 'the world's northernmost town' and the departure point for boat trips to the North Cape before roads were built. (Photo: TO-FOTO)

In 1891, Hammerfest became the first town in Norway to have electric street lighting and its own power station. Its strategic location made it a natural choice for the base of the German fleet during the sea war in the North Atlantic, between 1940 and 1944. It was razed to the ground by General Rendulic in 1944 and has since been rebuilt as a modern town. Tourist traffic to the North Cape has had a positive effect on local business, and local hopes are being pinned on the huge gas finds made in the North Arctic Ocean and the Barents Sea. Around 120 km. To the northwest lie the oilfield Snøvit and the gas fields Albatross and Askeladden. Oil and gas from the fields will be transported by boat to a terminal on Melkøy just north of Hammerfest harbour. From there they will be shipped by sea to customers in mainland Europe. 58 km of road and a magnificent suspension bridge connect the town to the E6 and, every year, 95,000 passengers pass through Norway's busiest short strip airport. The local newspaper has 12,000 subscribers. Turbines are being installed on the seabed in Kvalsundet east of the town. They are driven by the tide-run, and generate electric power.

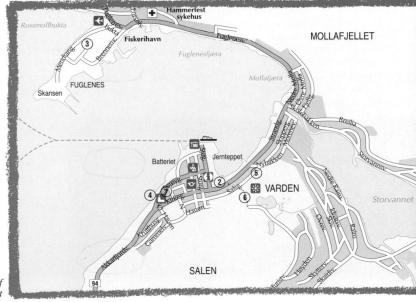

Town map of Hammerfest

What to do in Hammerfest.
1. **Shopping** is a traditional activity. The widespread belief that polar bears roam the streets of Norway originated in Hammerfest. A heavyweight example of the species can usually be seen outside one of the shops in the town, and is a constant source of delight to visiting photographers.
2. A visit to **the Polar Bear Club (Isbjørnklubben)** is a must. Here you can see historical collections of exhibits from the town's Arctic and trapping past, as well as a collection of stuffed birds. Admission is free. The club has 193,000 members,

but is more than willing to accept more. Your proof of membership is an ornate certificate, giving you the right to wear a polar bear badge in your buttonhole!

3.   **The Meridian Marker** at Fuglenes, erected on the same site as the 1809 defences. The marker commemorates the joint project to determine the size and shape of the globe carried out by Russia, Norway and Sweden between 1816 and 1852.

4.   The entire end wall of **Hammerfest Church** is a spectacular stained glass window. The crypt is the only building in the town to have survived World War II.

5.   **St. Michael's Church** is a Roman Catholic church built mainly by German volunteers. A 10,000 piece mosaic portrays St. Michael and the dragon.

6.   **Salen Restaurant**, 80 m above sea level, offers a panoramic view of the surrounding area

7.   **Gjenreisingsmuseet** [the Museum of Reconstruction] shows how the region was rebuilt after General Rendulic's total destruction in 1944.

As we sail south we pass **Sørøya**, Norway's fourth largest island, to the west. The island has been populated since the Stone Age and the remains of a Dutch whaling station can also be seen here. The island is most heavily populated on the southern side, in the fishing villages of Hasvik (650 inhabitants), Breivikbotn (450 inhabitants), and Sørvær (350 inhabitants). 6,000 passengers pass through Hasvik Airport every year.

Sørøya became famous in 1944. The population refused to evacuate to southern Norway when German troops withdrew. A total of 1,000 people escaped to large caves and watched as the village was razed to the ground. They lived under appalling conditions until they were rescued, by both Norwegian and British vessels. Some were taken to Båtsfjo1rd and some to England. The caves are still accessible.

The open sea has always held a great attraction for us humans.
(Photo: Ola Røe)

To the east we see the large island of **Seiland**, where you can glimpse the relatively small glaciers of Nordmannsjøkulen (1,075 m above sea level) and Seilandsjøkelen (981 m above sea level). During the summer, the Kautokeino Sami live here with their reindeer. Further southeast lies the island of **Stjernøya**. In Lillebukt, you will see the rare nepheline mines which produce around 230,000 tonnes of nepheline syenite ore per year for the glass industry. The workers live in Alta and commute by boat. The Kautokeino Sami also graze their reindeer here.

Travel to Alta by road or air to see a worldwide attraction: the rock carvings at Hjemmeluft. (Photo: Jon M. Fjeldstad)

Alta Fjord cuts 30 km inland to what is the most densely populated area of Finnmark, due to its forests and mild climate. This is the furthest north that grain can grow - and ripen. The municipality of Alta has 17,000 inhabitants.

The 19th century mining activities are a major part of the area's history, and the large Alta slate quarries are also well known. During the war, Alta was a safe haven for the German battleships 'Scharnhorst' and 'Tirpitz', until two British midget submarines seriously damaged 'Tirpitz' in 1943. The «Scharnhorst» was sunk on Christmas Day 1943, North of the North Cape. In 1973, over 2,500 rock carvings and settlements dating back as much as 9,000 years were discovered here. The prize-winning Alta Museum has been built around the carvings which are on the UNESCO World Heritage List, as are the pyramids of Egypt. As early as 1899/1900 the renowned Professor Kristian Birkeland built an Aurora Borealis observatory on the peak of Hallde (907 m above sea level). On the island of Årøy you can still see the remains of Christian IV's fortifications dating from 1609. They were built as a defence against the Swedes. The Coastal Express does not call at Alta, but you can reach it by road (E6) or by air (200,000 passengers per annum). When you get there, try salmon fishing in the Alta River and see the most controversial hydroelectric scheme in Norway.

ØKSFJORD is not the southernmost port of call in Finnmark, as both Kirkenes and Vadsø are further south. You are, in other words, still above 70° north. Trading began in 1814, and although fishing has always taken place here, it was the arrival of huge herring shoals during the 19th century that led to the town's growth. The district has a population of 800 and is the administrative centre for the municipality of Loppa with its population of 1,400. A 40 km road links Øksfjord to the E6 highway and a number of local ferries (car ferries) serve Hasvik on Sørøya Island and other destinations. Clearly the area is dependent on the fishing industry. It has fish processing plants and - of course - a ship-yard. To the southeast you can glimpse Norway's fifth largest glacier, Øksfjordjøkulen (1,204 m above sea level). This is the only glacier on mainland Norway to 'calve' direct-ly into the sea, although this takes place out of the view of Coastal Express passengers at the head of Jøkel Fjord, to the south of the peninsula. The author, Marie Corelli, wrote a best-selling book, 'Thelma' or 'The Norwegian Princess', about a 17 year old girl called Philippa from Øksfjord. This true story tells of a faithful English naval officer who returned, 5 years after his first visit, to marry her and take her back to London, where she was a great success in society.

There are several glaciers in northern Norway, but only Øksfjordjøkulen 'calves' into the sea, forming icebergs. (Photo: Ola Røe)

Lopphavet is one of six stretches öf open sea that the Coastal Express crosses. On the mainland you can see a number of small communities served by local ferries from Øksfjord. The Coastal Express often enters Berg Fjord to meet smaller boats. To the west is the island of Loppa, with its church. During the summer there is rich pollack fishing from the rocks and you can stay at a boarding house here. Legend has it that, in 1860, a wealthy English hunter, Mr White, wanted to lease the hunting rights here. The Tromsø solicitor handling the affair did not, however, have a very good grasp of English and sold the island for 2,000 dollars, making the island formally English property until 1890. We then cross the mouth of **Kvænangen Fjord**, which is 70 km long. The name comes from 'kven', a name for the Finns, and 'angr' meaning fjord. Traces of the so-called 'Komsa' people's most southwesterly settlements have been discovered here. These people inhabited an area which stretched from here through Alta, eastern Finnmark to Varanger and then in through the coastal areas of the White Sea in Russia. To the west, there are fishing villages and bird colonies on the large islands of Arnøy and Laukøy, which have a good road network and a car ferry connecting them to the municipal centre of Skjervøy.

SKERVØY is a natural harbour situated between the mountain ranges and deep fjords which stretch into the great expanse of the Norwegian Sea. The area has a new tunnel (2,095 m long) and a road to the E6 highway which winds along the coasts of Lyngen Fjord, Reisa Fjord and the mighty Kvænangen. The municipality of Skjervøy has a population of 3,900.

Fishery has been the basic source of income here for time immemorial. The community still lives on the proceeds of fishing and processing, together with ship repairs and the production of aquaculture equipment. Certain ancient Sami settlement sites found here date back to the Stone Age. Skjervøy is a traditional trading centre, owned by one family for long periods, and legends about the king of Skervøy still abound. He lived 300 years ago and was called Christen Michelsen Heggelund. The author priest, Petter Dass, has written a number of enjoyable stories about this somewhat heavy-handed and colourful trader who ruled the local community. The most famous of these tales tells of when he confiscated the local church's collection as a part of his financial dealings with the local priest, who was somewhat sceptical about his kingdom.

Skervøy is also famous for being the first port of call, in August 1896, of the polar vessel 'Fram' which had been absent for 3 years on Nansen's expedition to the North Pole. Everyone had eagerly anticipated news of the fate of 'Fram', especially since Nansen and Johansen, who had left 'Fram' in the Arctic Sea, had arrived in Vardø a week earlier.

We have left Lopphavet behind us and are now heading for Tromsø. You can read about this stretch under Day 5. If you are lucky with the weather between May and July, you may see the Midnight Sun shining off Fjellheisen peak in Tromsø. During the rest of the year, weather permitting, you may see the Northern Lights or the magical play of the moon on the sea.

See day 5 for Tromsø.

N
W   E
S

Hvalsafari

Andenes
Bleiksøya   Andøya Flyatsjon
Bleik

Nordmela   Ramså
    Andfjorden
Dverberg

Andøya   Helløya
   Senja

Anda Fyr   Åse   Bjarkøy   Vå
Risøyhamn   Grøtavær   Sandsøya

Øksnes   Myre Alsvåg   Elgsnes   Grytøya

VESTERÅLEN   Toppsundet

Nykan   Langøya   Kvæfjord   Kvæfjord   Trondenes K.
    Roll.

Sortland   Harstad
Straume   Kleiva   Flesnes   Revsnes   Kilbotn
   Sigerfjord   sldsundet

Litløy Fyr   Bø   Skagen   H n n ø y a   Evenskjer
  Vesterålsfjorden   Kongsvik

Hadseløya   Stokmarknes   Møysalen   Ramsund   Lil
   Melbu   *1262
   Hadselfjorden   Hadsel   Evenes

    Trollfjorden   Lødingen   Ofotf
     Ofotfjorden   Ballangen   Bjørk

Eggum   Gimsøy   Austvågøy
   Svolvær Lufthavn   Svolvær   Brettesnes   Tranøy Fyr   Stetinden
Vestvågøy   Vågakallen   Kabelvåg   *1392
Flakstadøy   942 *   Skrova Fyr   Hamsund   Kjøpsvik
   Leknes   Henningsvær   Hamarøy
Fredvang   Gravdal Stamsund   Moholmen Fyr
  Ramberg   Ure
Sund   Mortsund   Henningsværstraumen   Skutvik
   Nusfjord   Ballstad
   Nesland
   Mølnarodden   Flatøy Fyr   Sagfjorden
Moskenes   Hamnøy   Engeløya
  Reine   Grøtøy   E6
Tind   Sørvågen   Steigen   Tysfjorden
Å   Leinesfjord

Moskenesstraumen   Leiranger

VESTFJORDEN   Skarholmen Fyr   Folda
Værøy   Sørland   Måløy
  Værøy Fyr

Røsthavet   Kjerringøy   Sørfolda   E6
Nykan   Røst   Røsvik
Skomvær Fyr   Rago
    Nasjonalpark

   Landegode Fyr   Straumen
Heligvær   S a l t e n

Tennholmen Fyr   Strømsnes
  Bliksvær   Bodø   Løding   Fauske
  Bodø Lufthavn   Skjerstad   Suliskongen
   Saltfjorden   Saltstraumen   *1907
Arnøy   Sulithjelma
Sandhornøy   Rognan

HARSTAD was described under Day 4. Today, you'll have the opportunity to see some of the sights you missed out on, on our journey north.

We board the ship again and savour the journey northwards, passing Trondenes church, the former court and seat of one the most influential families during the Viking era. Trondenes should be viewed from the sea, as it was in the past.

Next we see a fort and the Adolf Gun high up on a hill, but don't worry: it is not loaded, and it takes a while to transport the shells by rail and lifts from the arsenals which still exist today. As we enter the Toppsundet strait, we see the tiny island of Kjeøya with its rock paintings to the south. Say goodbye to Harstad!

At the end of the strait lies Elgsnes, with its burial mounds, sacrificial sites and a memorial chapel to Greenland's apostle, Hans Egede (see under Harstad church). Also to be found here is Grøtavær (250 inhabitants), a fishing village where many Iron Age relics have been discovered.

Next we head for Risøyrenna - a dredged channel between the islands of Hinnøya and Andøya. Before 1922 the Coastal Express had to sail into Tjeldsundet strait, leaving the whole of Vesterålen (ål=sea) alone to the west. See the chart, page 129.

The Coastal Express enters historical waters in Toppsundet. To the east is Trondenes, to the north the islands of Bjarkøy and Grytøya, rich in Iron Age findings. Elgsnes, to the west, boasts former sacrificial sites and burial mounds. To the southwest, Kvæ Fjord is an agricultural area, famous for its strawberries. (Photo: TO-FOTO)

Andøya is a curious island. 5,700 inhabitants and a newspaper with 2,300 subscribers. Naturally, it has mountains, but the side of the island closest to the mainland consists mainly of. lowlands. The area has enormous peat bogs, cloudberry marshes and coal deposits (not commercially viable). The mine at Ramså is popularly known as 'The open geology book'. It consists of 300 km thick deposits of sandstone containing coal under layers of sandstone and shale as well as the complete skeletons of ichthyosaurs, enormous fish-like dinosaurs which roamed the area 150 million years ago. Norwegians arrived much later, and burial mounds as well as the remains of former Iron Age settlements tell their own story. Furthest to the north, Andenes, the capital, has 3,500 inhabitants and dates back to 1300. The town is built around the site of a single huge farm. Fishing has always been the main industry here, although when the fishing industry suffered a setback along the coast during the 1600s, Andenes survived as a supply base for Dutch whalers. Today, 'whale safaris' are a major attraction, offering trips to see the elegant 20 m long, 40 tonne, sperm whales. On the coast, a NATO airbase of great strategic importance has been built. Many nations launch their research rockets and balloons from «Oksebåsen» There are several bird colonies in the area, one of which, Bleik, is the nesting place for at least 160,000 puffins:

Whale safaris off the coast of Andenes, observe the 20 m long, 40 tonne 'stars'. These whales are twice the length of the minke whales mentioned on pages 98-99. (Photo: Knudsens Fotosenter)

We have now passed **RISØYHAMN,** (350 inhabitants), which was a prosperous trading post around 1777. The islands of Hinnøya and Andøya are linked by a 750 m bridge. Heading south, with Hinnøya to the east and Andøya to the west, we pass yet another large island, Langøya. After about an hour, another bridge (961 m long) comes into view. This bridge links Hinnøya and Langøya on the E10 highway between Narvik/Bjerkvik and Lofoten.

SORTLAND has 4,000 inhabitants and is the main town of Vesterålen. The 3 municipalities on Langøya have a total of 17,000 inhabitants. Around half of these live on the island's west side. From here, there are roads leading to the rich fishing villages and historical sites (Bø and Øksnes/Myre). The herring years in the second half of the last century prompted growth which in turn led to the development of modern fishing fleets and a processing industry. Fish offal is used industrially in oils, enzymes and proteins for the cosmetic, pharmaceutical and health industries.

The Norwegian author, Knut Hamsun, was a sheriff's servant in Bø as a boy. Sortland is featured in the Sagas. This was also the home of Karle and Gunnstein who accompanied Tore Hund to Russia (see Bjarkøy, Day 5). There were prosperous trading centres here around 1781. In addition to being involved with widespread trade, the area had a canning factory, fishing boat company, concrete goods factory, dairy and slaughterhouse. The local newspaper, "Bladet Vesteraalen" has 10,700 subscribers .

Sortland is the headquarters of Norway's coastguard. They patrol vast areas of the North Atlantic five times larger than mainland Norway. A few years ago, the Norwegian coastguard rescued hundreds of cruise passengers to the west of Svalbard. The best-known ships are the ones which, together with the coastguard's Orion planes, protect Norwegian waters, the protected area around Svalbard, and huge areas in the Barents Sea including 'Gråsonen' [the Grey Zone] and 'Smutthullet' [the Loophole] (see the section on fishing borders and the Continental Shelf). First-time visitors to Vesterålen will be surprised to see the green stripe of agricultural land which stretches from the coast to the mountain range further inland. The islands resemble hats with green hat brims. Iron Age names are still in use here (from before the Viking era): Hov (heathen place of   sacrifice), Bø, Vik etc.

Next we head for Stokmarknes. To the north, we see the 1,020 m long bridge which links the islands of Langøya and Hadseløya. (It is provided with an audio barrier which prevents foxes from spreading to Hadseløya). North of the bridge is Skagen airport which handles almost 90,000 passengers every year. There is certainly no cause for complaint over the lack of bridges and means of communication.

STOKMARKNES (3,500 inhabitants) is the administrative centre for Hadseløya's 8,300 inhabitants and has been a prosperous trading post since 1776. Between 1850 and 1939, it was the venue for a large annual summer market for people living on the coast of Helgeland and Vesterålen. The area has fish and shrimp processing facilities as well as lumber yards and a large hospital. 2,900 people subscribe to the local newspaper.

Visit the unique **Museum of the Coastal Express** here. This is where Richard With, the Coastal Express' founding father, established Vesteraalens Dampskibsselskab in 1881.

The rock at the old church site at Hadsel serves as an excellent sea mark, with its white, flat top resembling a sail (the Hofda sail). A large mound suggests that this was probably the seat of a former chieftain, and the first of the four churches that were built on this site was no doubt extremely old. To the south lies Melbu (2,500 inhabitants) which was an important estate during the Saga era. Today, a large number of enterprising trawlers and fish companies are based here and a major cultural event is held here every summer.

We head southeast, seemingly straight for the wall of a mountain. However, the captain knows his way and steers us skilfully through **Raftsundet**, a 20 km long strait which forges miraculously through the rocks between Hinnøya and Austvågøy (Vesterålen and Lofoten).
See the chart on page 128. Lofotveien crosses the sound to the mainland.The peaks tower 1,000 m above sea level and, weather permitting, something very special awaits us here.

Norwegian trolls had several fjords to choose from to call their own. They opted for Troll Fjord.
Thousands of passengers on the Coastal Express would agree with their choice. (Photo: TO-FOTO)

Troll Fjord is 2 km long and only 100 m wide at its mouth on the west side of Raftsundet. It is easy to let your imagination run riot here. To the south, the peak of Trolltindan soars 1,045-1,084 m above sea level, and its sheer sides pose a permanent threat of rock falls. To the north is Blåfjellet, rising 998 m above sea level. To the west and 162 m above sea level is the lake of Trollfjordvatnet, fills with chunks of ice even during the summer. This is the closest the Coastal Express can get to the Norwegian trolls. Don't worry, the captain knows the way out. He also knows that the trolls sleep for 1,000 years after their midday nap and before they start throwing stones at the ship.

Troll Fjord is famous for the Battle of Troll Fjord which took place here in 1880. The battle was between fishermen in steam-driven fishing boats and fishermen in 'fembøringer' (boats with sails and oars for five oarsmen). Huge quantities of fish had swum into the fjord and the fishermen in the larger boats were trapping them in a seine formed from their fishing nets, to the exasperation of the crews on the smaller boats.

The battle is described in Johan Bojer's novel 'The last Viking' and depicted in Gunnar Berg's painting 'The Battle of Troll Fjord', which hangs in Svolvær Town Hall.

Before we begin our approach to Svolvær, we pass the old fishing village of Skrova.

Svolvær is the capital of Lofoten. Mountain climbers jump between the horns of the 'Svolvær goat'. (Photo: Aune Forlag)

SVOLVÆR remains the undisputed capital of Lofoten, despite the fact that Kabelvåg/Vågan was the historical centre. You can't mistake Svolværgeita ['Goat mountain'] with its two noticeable horns 1.5 m apart. Daring adventurers have been known to jump from one to the other.

Svolvær has 4,000 inhabitants and the municipality has 9,200. The world's largest catches of cod, made here between January and April, were the reason for the development of this small coastal town. The average catch was 40-50 million kg. Now the catch varies from year to year, ranging between 25-50 million kilos. Today, there are less than 3,000 fishermen compared with 20,000 in 1947. The town has a number of industries, all linked to fish processing, fishing itself and boat traffic.There are great expectations connected with the production of cod and halibut juveniles for the aquaculture industry.

'Atlantic cod - the cod has made many a man happy'. (Petter Dass in his description of Lofoten). (Photo: Samfoto, Hans Hvide Bang)

Svolvær is not just a centre for fishing. In addition to fishermen, the winter streets are full of skiers on their way to the winter sports centre, as well as artists who flock here for the local scenery, the colourful street life and, perhaps more than anything else, the light. A circle of artists has developed since the last century, and the Vågan Artistic Centre and Art House have been set up. Like Gunnar Berg (1863-1893) and his painting 'The Battle of Troll Fjord', other well-known painters have also been inspired by Lofoten: Werenskiold, Kittelsen, Revold and Rolfsen. Today, Kåre Espolin Johnson and Karl Erik Harr are the best known. A large number of paintings are displayed on board the Coastal Express ships.

The influx of tourists has meant the development of a reliable range of services and attractions for travellers. There are plenty of hotels in the area. The airport serves approximately 68,000 passengers per year. Lofotposten has approximately 9,400 subscribers. Over 12,000 people subscribe to Lofotposten, the local newspaper. Temperatures in the area are neither particularly high nor low. The average temperature in July is + 13.9° C and + 1.8° C in

January. As we make our way south, Skrova lighthouse flashes to the east. There is considerable cod fishing and salmon farming around **Skrova** (400 inhabitants). Skrova is also home to a marine biological research station, founded by G.O. Sars, the founder of Norsk fiskeriforskning [Norwegian Research into Fisheries]. Based on the results of this research, Skrova's inhabitants decided to continue the traditional way of life of past generations, i.e. whaling. The people of Skrova believes that the results of the research carried out by the International Whaling Commission's Science Committee must count more than emotions.

Lighthouses are an integral part of life on the coast. Even though modern instruments demonstrate startling precision, it is comforting to see the flashing lights wishing us a safe journey. (Photo: Ola Røe)

To the west and just south of Svolvær lies **Kabelvåg/Storvågan.Vågan church**, Lofoten Cathedral, is the largest wooden church in the north, with a seating capacity of 1,200. During the Lofoten fishing boom, the church always had a full congregation. King Eystein built the area's first church during his visit in 1120 and a statue has been erected in his memory.

Kabelvåg (2,000 inhabitants). A former centre for Hålogaland, King Håkon Håkonson made Kabelvåg the trade centre of the North. Storvågan is close by, and excavation work carried out here suggests that this was the trade centre for Hålogaland (c. 1100-1400). This was possibly the country's third market town. In the Middle Ages, Bruraberget was the site of courts and the Vågåbok book of laws originated here. It is due to Lofoten fishing that the area flourished some 900 years ago, and now is home to the Lofoten aquarium and Lofoten Museum.

In Borge, about 60 km. from Svolvær, a Viking Chieftain's farm has been excavated. The Banqueting Hall and the ship have been restored as a museum, showing daily life, clothing and more.

Vågekallen is the 'king' of Lofoten. He was not always made of stone. Read about his exploits in the Saga of the Helgeland Mountains under Day 10.
(Photo: TO-FOTO)

Vågekallen (942 m above sea level) behind Henningsvær should be treated with respect. According to tradition, a "first tripper", a marine term for a sailor on his first voyage, in the Lofoten fishing fleet had to remove his hat and greet Vågekallen. Today, it serves as a good sea mark. The demanding ascent takes three and a half hours and the mountain was first conquered in 1885. Moholmen lighthouse can be seen flashing nearby.

Henningsvær is spread across several small islands further out to sea. This fishing village has been formed by nature. A local saying is 'I'm a real Lofoten cod, because I was born in Henningsvær'! In the past, everyone could row a boat, and the islands' location was perfect. Today, however, bridges are required to reach the islands and the E10 highway. The 750 permanent residents run fishing factories and produce dried, salted fish, cod roe, 'Lofotpostei' sandwich spread and fillets of fish. Rows and rows of fishermen's cabins are to be found here. Art has also made its arrival here, not least in the form of Karl Erik Harr's art gallery.

Henningsværstraumen is the stretch of sea between Henningsvær and Stamsund. The paths of the northbound and southbound Coastal Expresses usually cross here.

*Today, cars have replaced boats as the usual means of travel between Henningsvær and the countless small islands. Bridges have been built, and the place has become a popular tourist destination.
(Photo: Helene Winsents)*

STAMSUND (1,300 inhabitants) is a man-made fishing village defiantly built into the mountainside. J.M. Johansen initiated the construction of the village during the first half of the 1900s. This is now one of Lofoten's largest fishing villages and has excellent quay facilities, one of Lofoten's largest fish product plants, a cod liver oil refinery and its own shipping company with 7 trawlers. Stamsund's main products became dried cod and guano. In addition to hotels, there are a large number of fishermen's cabins available. To the west and close to the main E10 highway, roads past the fishing villages are winding, but good. Leknes, the centre, also lies at the heart of Vestvågøy Island, with its 10,700 inhabitants. It has an airport which caters for more than 75,000 passengers a year. The local newspaper has 4,500 subscribers. After Flakstad and Moskenes, the E10 to Å is free of ferries. With the exception of Værøy Island and Røst, the remaining outlying areas remain relatively untouched. For further information on Lofotveggen, Vest Fjord and the fishermen's cabins, see Day 4.

Whaling and seal hunting have been an important part of the basis for existence of humans on the Norwegian coast since pre-historic times. In recent times, international organs have established scientific commissions to ensure that both whales and fisher-folk have a future.

A key phrase is "sustainable development", which protects the environment, the stocks of living species and provides the potential for man to reap renewable resources.

At certain periods in the 1980's, and to the consternation of the fishermen, large numbers of seals from northern waters came into Norwegian waters. Firstly, the seals periodically destroyed the natural resource base and secondly they also destroyed the nets. Norwegian authorities are now preparing legislation for controlled hunting of coastal seals.

With regard to the larger species of whales, which were the victims of industrial whaling for the production of whale oil, this chapter in history is now closed. Many of these magnificent large mammals now swim undisturbed in Norwegian waters. The official Norwegian view however is that whale should be hunted in a sustainable manner in the same way as other marine species.

There is a total of around 75 species of whale. Five of these have been severely over hunted and twelve are considered to be at risk. It is different for the minke whale, which is the whale still hunted by Norway. It is the smallest of the baleen whales and reproduces faster than any other whale species.

In 1982 the International Whaling Commission, of which Norway is an active member, introduced a general moratorium on commercial whaling. According to this resolution, new quotas were to be allotted by 1990 at the latest. However, thus far (2002) this has not been done. Norway reserved itself against the resolution and is therefore – pursuant the Commission's own rules – not bound by it.

Within the framework of the Whaling Commission's Science Committee, Norway carried out surveys over a five year period. In 1992, the Science Committee unanimously concluded that stocks of minke in the north-east Atlantic were between 61,000-117,000 animals. Later surveys have estimated the figure to be around 112,000. In addition, the mid-Atlantic stock is in the region of 72,000 (this is the stock hunted by Norway in the waters around Jan Mayen). On the basis of accepted calculating principals, the Atlantic stock is large enough to allow limited hunting. The minke is found in all the world's oceans. In the Antarctic alone there are probably in the region of 750,000 animals.

However, the bulk of the Whaling Commission's member countries still adhere to the principal of total protection of all species of whales. This conflicts with the Commission's own Science Committee's report.

Against this background, Norway resumed limited whaling of the minke whale in 1993. See under Risøyhamn on the whale safari at Andenes (Andøya, Day 9).

Aqua culture. Fish farming.

Passengers on the Coastal Express can often see the sea farming plants along the coast. There are in the region of some 3,000 such plants. During recent years, the plants have come to represent a new and thriving industry after a few "teething troubles" have been overcome. Quality is now extremely high thanks to intensive research and experience.

Salmon is the king amongst aqua culture species, and can be found in restaurants around the globe. Production has increased to in excess of 420,000 tonnes. Trout is also popular, with annual production reaching 45,000 tonnes. Scientists are also working on improving the quality of cod, halibut, sea urchin, char, eel, wolf fish and mussels, but production is still relatively low as yet.

The value of exports of farmed fish has passed 10 billion Norwegian kroner per annum. This represents one-third of the value of all fish and seafood exports. While conventional fishing at sea is limited by international quotas, the sea farming industry can continue to increase its production.

N
W E
S

Landego
Helgvær
Tennholmen Fyr
Bliksvær
Bodø
Bodø Lufthavn
Saltfjorden

VØRINGBASSENGET

Arnøy
Sandhornøy
Fugleøya
Gildeskål Kirke
Inndyr
Bei

Tennholmfjorden
Kalsholmen Fyr
Støtt
Kunna
Høgnakken
1045

Ørnes

Myken Fyr
Meløy
Bolga
Grønøy
Glomfjord
Amøy
Holandsfjorden

Rødøyløva
440
agsfjorden
Engabreen
Istind
1572

Nesøya
Gjerøya
Snøtind
1599
Svartisen

Hestmannøy
Ringsundøya
568
Hestmona

Træna
POLARSIRKEL

TRÆNABANKEN
Træna Fyr
Trænfjorden
Lurøy
Stroforshei

Lovunden
Lovund
Krigskirkegård
E

Åsvær Fyr
Utskarpen
Mo i Rana

Tømma
Ranafjorden
Hemnesberget

Svale
Dønnes Kirke
Nesna
Finneidfjord

Norne
Hugla
Løkta
Bjerka

Dønna
Korgen

Ytterholmen Fyr
Dønnmannen
Bjørn
Seløy
858
Sandnesjøen
E6

Herøy
Alstenøy
Stokka
Sju Søstre
Okstindan
1916

Sandnessjøen Lufthavn
Alstahaug
1072
Velsnfjorden

Krigskirkegården
Skarv
Hotta
Mosjøen

Mindlandet
Røsvatn

Stokkefjorden

Gladstad
Vevelstad

Vega
Ylvingen
E6

Bremstein Fyr
Hattfjelldal

VELFJORDEN
Tilrem
Skaren
Velfjorden
Trofors

Brønnøysund

SKLINNABANKEN
Torghatten
Trolnæs
Holmestø
Berg

Tosentunnelen

Sønna

Sklinna Fyr
Kvigtinden
1699

Horta
Vennesund
Bindalsholmen
Holm
Tosenfjorden
Børgefjell
Nasjonalpark

Leka
Gutvik
Sølsemhulen
Terråk

Lysøya
Fingarshulen
Risvær
Gjerdinga
E6

100 Fyr
Vikna
Foldereid
Indre Foldafjorden
Røyrvik
Rørvik
Ottersøy
Kolvereid
Nærøy
Nærøyfjorden

From the Arctic Circle to Rørvik

Witness the amazing coastline between Ørnes and the Arctic Circle during the day (or morning) on the southbound and northbound Coastal Express. Read Day 4 for further information on this leg of the journey, which passes 1,000 islands and skerries, shrouded by Svartisen's luminous mantle to the east. Today, our account begins in the morning as we cross the Arctic Circle, leaving behind the Land of the Midnight Sun.

We have a wonderful day ahead of us, sailing down the Helgeland coast. Look to the east, in the direction of Mel Fjord and Svartisen glacier. To the west is our old friend, Hestmannen Island. Beyond it you can just about make out the island group of **Træna** (550 inhabitants) riddled with bird colonies and caves, in which remains of 5,000-year old settlements have been found. Perhaps you can also make out Træna lighthouse in the distance. Next, we see the island of **Lurøy** to the west. It is the location of a 200-year old estate and unique Renaissance garden, which belonged to the Scottish Dundas family. (Petter Dass' family also hailed from here). Further to the west is Lovunden with its 100,000 puffins. We sail west passing between large islands. For the rest of today, we will be passing a belt of skerries and small islands interspersed with fishing villages. Next, we turn towards **NESNA** - an idyllic and tranquil former trading post (950 inhabitants). The municipality has 1,900 inhabitants. A rural museum and old vicarage can also be visited here. Unfortunately, we do not stop long enough here for you to take a walk.

Rana Fjord stretches 70 km inland to the industrial town of Mo i Rana (25,000 inhabitants) which has former iron mines and a number of interesting mountain caves which are accessible to tourists.

Dønna. On the island of Løkta lies the former trading post of Kopardal (now a ferry stop). The large island of Dønna dominates to the west. 1,600 people live on this historical island. In the far north of the island is the unique Dønnes church, linked to the Dønnes estate by a shared past stretching from the Saga era to the present day. The estate belonged to the Coldewin family. The brick church dates back to the 1200s and has secret underground passages. For a long time, many people believed that it was a fortress church. The Coldewin family's burial chamber contains embalmed bodies. 500 coins have been found under the floor, some dating from the time of Håkon Håkonson (1200s). On the east coast of Dønna is the market town of Bjørn (now a ferry harbour). In the past, there were 160 stalls here, and up to 3,000 people visited the place in their boats in July. The new Bjørnmarkedet on the 2nd weekend in July now attracts several thousand visitors.

SANDNESSJØEN. You could not wish for a more perfect location. To the west, Dønnamannen Mountain, 858 m above sea level, towers above the islands. To the east, the modern architecture of the elegant Helgeland Bridge impresses visitors. It measures more than 1,100 m in length and has a main span of 395 m. It cost almost NOK 395 million to build. The bridge spans Leir Fjord which flows into Vefsn Fjord. This, in turn, leads towards the industrial town of Mosjøen (13,000 inhabitants), 70 km away.

Torolv Kvedulvsson, a Viking chieftain of the Saga era, lived at Sandnessjøen (on the Sandnes farm). He collected taxes from the Sami people for Harald Hårfagre, but became too powerful for the king's liking and paid with his life. Sandnessjøen has remained a centre of activity ever since. Today, the municipality has 7,500 inhabitants and a variety of industries and occupations such as fishing, agriculture(!), industry, trade and administration. Bustling ferry traffic has made the place a hive of activity. Oil and gas finds at

Norne bring hope and expectations of spin-off effects for local society. A local newspaper with 6,400 subscribers.

Herøy. Travelling south from Sandnessjøen, we pass the island of Herøy with its 1,800 inhabitants. The island has 5 bridges and Herøy church/'Helgeland's Cathedral' which dates back to the 1100s. On the island of Alsten is Sandnessjøen airport which handles around 50,000 passengers every year.

The 7 sisters. Raise your eyes and gaze at the impressive '7 sisters'. Let us introduce them from north to south: Botnkrona (1,072 m), Grytfoten (1,066 m), Skjæringen (1,037 m), Tvillingene (980 m), Kvasstinden (1,010 m), Stortinden (910 m). It is no wonder that these ladies have inspired local tales. Just listen to the folklore of the Helgeland mountains.

According to Norwegian folk tales, trolls are turned to stone if they do not hide before the sun rises. This was also the case for the 7 beautiful sisters who, as mountains, are still just as beautiful. (Photo: Samfoto, Kjell Karlsson)

The Saga of the Helgeland mountains: This is the story of a man called Vågekallen who lived in Lofoten, just beyond Henningsvær. He missed the company of women, as the ladies further south did not take much notice of him. In fact, Lekamøya even called him a simpleton. One night, when Lekamøya had gone to Tjøtta to make unleavened bread, something happened: 7 beautiful sisters had escaped from their father, the King of Sulitjelma, and were dancing naked in the fjord. The temptation proved too great for Vågekallen. He jumped on his horse and rode south in great haste causing a great deal of commotion. The 7 sisters fled southwards with Vågekallen hard on their heels. Lekamøya heard the din from where she was baking at Tjøtta. She dropped her rolling pin, peel and pastry board and set off home to Leka. Hestmannen was woken by the noise and shot an arrow south. However, Skarvågsgubben (the king of Brønnøy Island) saw this and threw up his hat to intercept the arrow which landed in the sea. They were all turned to stone as they forgot the sunrise, and can still be seen here to this day. From north to south: Vågekallen in Lofoten, Hestmannen on his horse and well guarded by the Rødøy Island Lion and the 7 sisters on Alsten. Today, the pastry board, rolling pin and peel are stone monuments at Tjøtta and the hole through the Brønnøy king's hat, 'Torghatten', can still be seen. Lekamøya stands at Leka. Just look and you'll find them all (even on the map).

Alstahaug. Alstahaug Church, dating from the 1100s and extended in 1865, is a prominent landmark on the southern tip of Alsten. The old churchyard has Norway's northernmost oak (4 m tall). The churchyard dating from 1650 has been beautifully restored. This is where the poet and priest, Petter Dass, (Dundas) earned his living in 1689. It was certainly a profitable living and Petter was careful with his money. He had his own fishing boats which transported fish to Bergen, and travelled round visiting his loyal parishioners.
Today, it is as a poet that he is famous in Norway. The verses flowed from his pen and, certainly, no-one else has captured northern Norway and the people here as well as he. His colourful masterpiece 'Nordlands Trompet' has become part of Norway's cultural heritage, as has the hymn 'Herre Gud ditt dyre navn og ære'. You will see his memorial on the headland north of the church. South of the church is a large royal grave, measuring 30 m in diameter and 8 m in height, which dates back to the Bronze Age. Chieftains resided here before the time of Petter Dass.

The War World II cemetery. A memorial bearing the Soviet star marks the beautiful grassy area where 7,551 Russian prisoners of war lie buried. This is also the burial site of 1,100 Russians, Germans, Czechs, Poles and Norwegians who died when the prison ship, Riegel, was accidentally bombed and sunk here. 2,578 prisoners died (compared with the 1,508 people who died when the Titanic sank).
Tjøtta. South of the war cemetery is **Tjøtta church**, situated in an area full of historical sites and Saga history. Hårek from Tjøtta was a great chieftain and one of St Olav's assassins at Stiklestad in 1030. Another well-known Saga character who lived here is the minstrel, Øyvind Finnson Skaldespiller (born in 912). Lekamøya's baking utensils (peel, pastry board and rolling pin) which were described in the Helgeland saga can also be found here. The peel, pastry board, rolling pin and dough. A farm site with the remains of 12 houses and 25 burial mounds in the shape of a star has also been unearthed here. Today, the estate itself on Tjøtta is northern Norway's largest. The government runs a sheep-breeding farm here, and carries out agricultural and maritime research in the area.

The large island of **Vega** lies to the west. 1,400 Norwegians live here on superb agricultural land, surrounded by fish and sea birds. Remains of former dwellings and burial mounds up to 10,000 years old have been found here. Excavations have yielded 280,000 artifacts and there are undoubtedly several more yet to be unearthed, so the locals need to be careful with their ploughs.

Høyholm. On the side of the mountain in the east we see a large white circle: "Opus for heaven and earth". It is constructed by Oddvar Daren as part of the project "Skulpturpark Nordland" (Sculpture Park Nordland), with works of art all over the entire county.

Tilrem. Until 1939, Tilrem, north of Brønnøysund was a market town. The foundations of St. Knuts church (1350) are covered by overgrown stones. The church was probably built by the Danish king, Knut den Eiegode, but some believe it was built by the English on the orders of King Harald Godwinson's brother in 1090-1100. Today, northern Norway's only vineyard, Hildurs Urterarium, is to be found here. The wine is served in a Saga hall in accordance with written consent from the state monopoly on wines and spirits - a fact not many people are aware of. Another little-known fact is that at Skåren you can see real cave paintings which are 4,000 years old.

BRØNNØYSUND, a small coastal town dating back to 1923, has 3,000 inhabitants. The municipality has 7,400 inhabitants and 4,800 people subscribe to the local newspaper. The airport handles almost 57,000 passengers every year. The narrow, but strategically situated harbour caters for all trade and fishing. The Stone Age settlements which have

Although Brønnøysund is situated in central Norway, it is still considered part of northern Norway.
(Photo: Trym Ivar Bergsmo)

been uncovered in the limestone caves at Sportsplassen tell their own story. The town has a mechanical workshop and a dairy and is also home to the Brønnøysund Registers (for companies, personal chattels, accounts and fees for the whole of Norway).

A 550 m long bridge leads over Brønnøysund Strait to an 8 km road running to the foot of Torghatten. From here, it is a half hour's walk to the hole in the mountain, 112 m above sea level. Weather permitting, passengers on the Coastal Express would of course prefer to see the hole from the sea, as is natural for seafarers (and in the past only seafarers visited the place). It is 160 m long, 25-30 m high and 12-15 m wide (25 m at the entrance). A fully-rigged Nordland fishing boat could easily get through here. Scientists claim that the sea washed against a weak point in the mountain, creating a hole, at the time when the land was some 100 m lower than it is today. Believe it if you want to. You will see clearly that it must have been Hestmannen's arrow which whisked through the Brønnøy king's hat so long ago when Lekamøya fled south!

Make sure you look east - the skeleton of a great auk has been found at Trælnes, opposite Torghatten. This flightless bird, which was as big as a goose is now extinct. Only 10 such

Torghatten has always been one of Norway's best-known natural phenomena.
(Photo: TO-FOTO)

skeletons exist in the world. It was once a cherished source of food for the local population. There are fertile agricultural areas to the south and the Sømna dairy is northern Norway's largest.

Central Norway. We are now as close to the heart of Norway as we can get. Scientists have calculated that Norway's geographical centre line passes through Tosen Tunnel on the route between Brønnøysund and the E6 highway. If, in the future, Norway becomes "the world's tunnel country", we will accept this decision. In "Fjord Country Norway", however, Bindal Fjord and Tosen Fjord mark the centre point of Norway with a deep fjord leading 60 - 70 km into the mountains. Almost simultaneously, we pass the border to

The Saga tells the story of Leka, as does the huge burial mound (15 m high and 55 m in diameter). But almost no-one knows that the 40 m long Solsem Cave at Leka has cave paintings depicting animals and swastikas.
(Photo: Samfoto, Jon Arne Sæter)

"Administrative Norway" between the counties of Nord-Trøndelag and Nordland. Far out at sea to the west, Sklinna lighthouse flashes above bird colonies and fishing grounds. North of Gurvik, to the east, the Fingals Cave conceals its cave paintings. Did you know that there are cave paintings in Norway?

To the west is **Leka**, a large island featured in the Sagas. 700 inhabitants. The red mountains are 500 million years old and were formed when the earth's crust erupted at the time when the continents were still connected. Historical sites dating back 10,000 years have been discovered here. The cave paintings (depicting animals and swastikas) are sensational and can also be found on the mainland, to the southeast. There is also a huge burial mound (55 m in diameter and 12 m tall) which is probably linked to the Saga king, Herlaug. In 1932, a 3-year old girl called Svanhild was carried away by an eagle and taken to its nest on a mountain, 300 m above the ground. She was later rescued and still lives in Rørvik. She has kept the dress she was wearing when she was taken. Gange-Rolv's mother was the daughter of a chieftain from Leka and is also an ancestor of the British Royal Family.

RØRVIK is the capital of a large island group called Vikna, which consists of almost 6,000 islets, skerries and islands and is populated by a myriad of birds. The area has spectacular fishing, fish farming and farming communities. Today, there are 3,700 inhabitants living on just seven of the islands. Njårdøy Island was a place of worship for Njård and a centre for Naumdøla County in the Saga era. This is also where Snorre Sturlasson's family lived.
The last recorded sighting of a sea serpent was made in 1926 by two boys fishing for mackerel on the northern side of Vikna, by Lysøya Island to the west of our route. The serpent was 200 m long and had 60 humps. Unfortunately, the boys did not have a camera with them.
Rørvik (The municipality has 3,800 inhabitants) lies in the middle of the route north/south and is characterised by services linked to shipping and sea-life. The town is also a busy trading and shopping centre. Things to visit in Rørvik include a fine coastal museum that is a centre of our national coastal culture and coastal industry and commerce, as well as exhibits of boats, a general store and a coffee bar. You have time for a visit while the Coastal Express is at the quayside. The high masts belong to the coast radio. The south-bound and northbound Coastal Express ships meet in Rørvik. Just south of the centre we'll see Marøysund Bridge, 600 m long, and Nærøysund Bridge, 700 m long with a central span of 325 m and a clearance of 41 m.
We then sail peacefully across Folla. Tomorrow we will wake up in Trondheim.

N
W   E
S

Njord

Kya Fyr

Buholmråsa Fy

Hepsøya

Kaura B
Bes

Værøya

Roan

FROHAVET

Finnvær Fyr

Harbakhulen
Stokkøya Harsvik
Linesøya Stokksund
Åsenvågøy Fyr

Afjord

Vingleia Fyr

Froan

Sula Mausund

Tarva Fyr

Lysøysund

Kjeungskjær Fyr

Botngård
Austrått Råkvagen

FRØYABANKEN

Titran Frøya

Sistranda
Hammarvika

Uthaug
Ørlandet

Brekstad

Veidholmen

Storfosna

Agdenes Fyr

Fillan

Hestvika

Reinskloster

Rissa

Lensvik

Vannvikan

Hitra

Jøsnøya
Hemnskjel

Sandstad

Selbekken

Ormen Lange

Smøla

Forsnes

Tjeldbergodden

Trondhei

Heimo

Grip Fyr

Edøy

Aure

Kyrksæterøra

Gjølme Børsa

Grip

Solskjeløya

Orkanger

Melhus

Kristiansund

Tustna

Årsundfjorden

Orkdal
Svorkmo

Kvål
Ler
E6
Lundamo

Kvitholmen Fyr

Kvernberget

Løkken

Hustadvika

Atlanterhavsveien

Averøya

Rindal

Storås

Hovin

Meldal

Støren

a Fyr

Bjørnsund

Bud

Eide

Surnadalsfjorden

Skei Surnadalsøra

Aa

Soknedal

GA

Elnesvagen

Gossen

ræna

Tingvoll

arøy

oft
ya

Otrøy

Hjelset

Molde

Molde lufthavn

Eidsvåg

Berkåk

Ulsberg

Brattvåg

Midsund

Veøy

Angy

Vestnes

Romsdalsfjorden

Langfjorden

Sunndalsfjorden

Sunndalsøra

vn
ad
elkavik

Vatne

Tomra

Skodje

Sjøholt

Andalsnes

Isfjorden

SUNNDALEN

Oppdal

Sykkylven

Romsdalshornet
1550

Eikesdalen

DOVREFJELL

Stordal

Romsdalen

Stranda

Trollstigen

Valldal

Tafjord

Snøhetta Dovrefjell
Nasjonalpark
2286

Hjerkinn

Hellesylt

Geiranger

Folldal

Strym
oen

Grotli

Dombås

Alve

Bismo

TRONDHEIM was a morning stop on the journey north. Read the description of this under Day 3. Some us didn't have time for a proper sightseeing tour of the town the first time around - as you can see from the description, there is plenty to see in this town! Nidaros Cathedral is part of Norway's national heritage with traditions linked to the whole of Catholic Europe. This is also where, together with the bishop of Nidaros, the Pope held Mass when he visited Norway in 1989. Today, we will visit the Cathedral and any other attractions we have time for. Greet the great Viking king, Olav Trygvason (995-1000), whose statue towers over the centre of town.

Trondheim (Nidaros) was the nation's capital. Nidaros Cathedral became the religious centre of Norway and a great international place of pilgrimage.
(Photo: Samfoto, Jon Arne Sæter)

We head out of the majestic Trondheims Fjord which is 170 km long and up to 25 km wide. Like all other Norwegian fjords it is deep, its greatest depth being 577 m. The outward journey is described under Day 3.Here you will be sailing directly over a gas pipeline on the seabed running from Haltenbanken to the gas driven power stations in Skogn/Levanger. (Which caused a crisis for the government).

Immediately before the fjord opens out towards the west, we see the former **Agdenes lighthouse** (1804 - 1894) on the headland to the west. Between 1895 and 1900, two coastal forts were built in this area, one here and another on the eastern side of the fjord. At the time, Norway was building up its military defences because the union with Sweden had crumbled. However, the guns were not used until the night of 8 April 1940, when a German warship suddenly and unexpectedly steamed over the horizon heading for Trondheim. The guns, which were more or less obsolete, were undermanned by the Norwegian neutrality guards. Very few shots rang out since the ships were out of firing range.

Agdenes lighthouse was built in 1804 and closed in 1984. The building is now a historical memorial with a superb view of the north side of the fjord looking across to Fosen Peninsula and Ørlandet.
(Photo: Knutsens Fotosenter)

Just west of the headland, King Øystein (1088-1123) built both a church and a mole. Many pilgrims, journeying across the sea to Nidaros, came ashore here in Hamn, as they were afraid of sea sickness caused by the powerful current in the fjord.

The so-called Trondheims Route to the south passes by the large island of Hitra to the west and Frøya further out to sea. The islands are linked to the mainland by large sub-sea road tunnels constructed in the seabed. The island of Hemnskjell, midway in the fairway is reached by a raised road which leads to a sub-sea tunnel, 5,800 metres long to Jøsenøya on Hitra. Another sub-sea tunnel, 4,800 metres long, runs from Hitra to Frøya.

Hitra has 4,000 inhabitants. There are fish and deer in the area and the Hitra salmon has won international acclaim. Sea fishing is carried out from the fishing villages on the coast of the island. There are several fish farms in the area and, in the 1970s, the recently established fish farming industry got off to a successful start with considerable exports of farmed salmon and trout. A coastal road has been built around the island, but further inland, in the forests and marshes, we find the kingdom of the deer. Hitra has possibly Europe's most dense stock of deer. The annual culling quota is large, and some 300 of these beautiful animals are shot every year. There were previously several smaller island communities at Frøya spread across the large banks and a chain of small islands on the Halten Bank.

Tjeldbergodden. On the mainland, just west of the county line between Sør-Trøndelag and Møre & Romsdal we find a large terminal at the end of a 245 km long pipeline carrying gas from Haltenbanken. The pipeline lies on the seabed where we have just sailed. It carries gas to the methane plant at Tjeldbergodden.

Smøla is another island chain out at sea with at least one skerry or one island for every one of Smøla's 2,400 inhabitants. There are significant agricultural and fishing activities on the low-lying island. On Edøy Island, close to our route, you will find Edøy stone church dating from around 1190. Just beyond Edøy is Kuløy Island with its many historical sites and graves. The runes on the Kuløy Stone date from around the time when Christianity was introduced into Norway and are very well known. The original stone is now on display at the University Museum in Trondheim and a replica has been erected on Kuløy Island. The construction of a windmill park on the island is a new project.

You are sure to enjoy
yourself on board the
Coastal Express.
(Photo: Nancy Bundt)

The magnificent mountain peaks of **Tustna**, rising some 900 m above the ground, stand out on the mainland. At the beginning of time, a crack in the earth's crust almost caused the islands to the west to sink into the sea, but the proud mountains at Tustna resisted. Harald Hårfagre won a great sea battle at Solskjel, against King Huntjov of Møre and King Nokkve of Romsdal. Both kings fell, but their sons were spared and returned to the same place the next year. Harald won again and Møre and Romsdal became his.

In the past, fishermen rowed out to the catch. It was important to live as close to the banks as possible. Grip is a charming example of this.
(Photo: Aune Forlag)

Surrounded by islets and skerries, **Grip** and the lighthouse soon comes into sight. In the 1960s, this was Norway's smallest municipality with 400 inhabitants, depleted to 135 inhabitants during the 1960's.Surrounded by the sea, clusters of houses have been built around a small stave church which dates back to 1470. The community has clung on here for centuries, even defying giant waves which, from time to time, have washed over the island. On two occasions only the church was left standing.

Although many people have holiday homes on Grip, this fishing paradise no longer has any permanent residents. Throughout the summer, a boat service runs to Kristiansund and the church is open. During the winter, however, only the lighthouse lights up the lonely countryside.

KRISTIANSUND is spread across three islands which are dependent on bridges and an excellent harbour. The place was originally called Fosna or Lille Fosen. The harbour was operational during the early Stone Age. The archaeologist Anders Nummedal has uncovered houses up to 10,000 years old, 40 metres above current sea level. He became a specialist on the Stone Age. These houses are a part of Fosna culture which is also familiar in other parts of the country.

Kristiansund's location has provided the town with a wealth of opportunities, and the town has shown an ability to adjust to fluctuations in the fishing, shipbuilding and oil industries. (Photo: Nancy Bundt)

On a number of occasions, the town has had to adapt to a constantly changing economy. It began in the 17th century, when the Dutch purchased timber here. Rights of self-government were granted in 1742, during the reign of Christian VI. The timber trade ceased, and was replaced by the herring industry. When the herring disappeared, cod (Atlantic cod) became the new product. 1691 saw the arrival of Jappe Ippes from Holland, often referred to as 'the founding father of 'klippfisk' [dried, salted cod]. He began drying and salting the cod on the bare, smooth, sloping rocks around the town, and Kristiansund soon became renowned for its dried, salted cod. Eventually, however, the Atlantic cod also let the town down, and fishermen had to travel to Lofoten for their catches, resulting in the need for boats. Activities spiralled until the Napoleonic Wars brought traffic to a halt.

In 1808, the town even had to defend itself against the English. The herring returned and the town flourished until World War I. The town's own ships transported dried, salted cod ('bacalao') to the Mediterranean countries. They used earth as ballast on the return journey which was collected for use in a churchyard. Although German bombers destroyed the town (724 houses) in April 1940, the new buildings have largely preserved the character of the town.

Town map of Kristiansund

The construction of an airport was important to the town, and today it handles some 270,000 passengers every year. In 1992, the town was at last linked to the mainland by a 5.2 km subsea tunnel and two huge bridges. The bill for these amounted to NOK 1 billion. The mainland town of Kristiansund has struggled to acquire a rather more varied industrial base. The most important industries are fishing, fish processing (the dried, salted fish is no longer dried on the rocks), refrigeration facilities and ship building. The town is also the base for the development of oil and gas on the Haltenbanken and is the operative base for the «Draugen» and «Heidrun» fields and the new, giant gas field «Ormen Lange». You will see the town and shipping traffic from the beacon tower outside of town. In the town itself, the "Sundferjene" serve to connect the different parts of town.

The town has 17,000 inhabitants and 15,000 people subscribe to the local newspaper.

Places to visit:
1. **Kristiansund church**. Rebuilt after the war, this is an unusual piece of architecture with an inventive design (the snow crystal) and beautiful stained-glass windows. (The leaning church).
2. **Nordlandet church** (1914) escaped the bombs in 1940 and Emanuel Vigeland's stained-glass windows remain intact.
3. **Nordmøre Museum**. Exhibits of Fosna culture, fishing industry, old wharves and boats.
4. **Milnbrygga** is Norway's Clipfish Museum.
5. **Three upper class homes** which survived the bombing of 1940.
6. **The Opera House.** The opera house Festiviteten, in characteristic Art Nouveau style. The town is well known for the operatic performances which culminate in February.
7. **Stone Age dwellings.**
8. **Grip (see above).**

With the delicious taste of bacalao still fresh in our minds, we head south of Hustavika. The stretch between Kristiansund and Molde, as well as the towns of Molde and Ålesund, are described under Day 2.

Out of the blue, Norway found itself with new natural resources. Oil and gas have replaced the old ore mines, which are now almost depleted. In 1968 a commercially viable oil field was discovered adjacent to the agreed demarcation line between Norway and Denmark/Great Britain. Production commenced in 1970. Oil exploration technology improved and activities moved further north. Deep-water technology allowed drilling and production at ever increasing depths.

Thirty years later Norway is now the world's 3rd largest oil exporter, and Norwegian gas supplies 10% of Europe's total gas consumption. The value of exports is now (dependent on oil prices) around 200 billion kroner annually. This is approximately 1/3 of Norway's total exports and 20 % of our gross national product.

Calculations show that approximately 22 % of presumed oil resources have already been recovered and that production will stagnate after 2004 and then go into decline. Gas production will increase, and will in all likelihood continue until the end of this century. Oil and gas exploration is going on in northern waters as far north as the Barents Sea to the demarcation line with Russia. However, the large continental shelf around Svalbard - a direct extension of the mainland Norwegian shelf - will no doubt remain untouched, and represents a potential treasure chest for future generations.

The first Norwegian oil fields lie south of Bergen, while the more recent fields are located in the seas to the west of the Coastal Express route. You won't be able to see the towering platforms, but you know that they are there, providing grounds for reflection over the riches this strange world of ours provides – and that are being consumed by our generation.

West of Bergen lie the Oseberg, Troll, Brage, Veslefrikk and other fields. You can see the land terminals for the oil pipes at Sture and the gas pipes at Kollsnes in Øygarden in the evening of day 1 and again on day 12 west of Herdla during the approach to Bergen and perhaps the Troll field to the west on the morning of the same day.

A little further north (west of Florø) lie the Statfjord, Gullfaks and Murchison fields. Statfjord lies on the dividing line between the British and Norwegian shelves. Income is distributed by neutral experts. This is how border disputes should be settled!

It's still "dry" between Florø and Kristiansund, but a new major gas field has recently been discovered west of Kristiansund (Ormen Lange). North of the Trondheimsfjord there are new fields like a string of pearls, including Njord, Draugen, Åsgard, Kristin, Heidrun and Norne. Norne is directly west of Sandnessjøen.

Travelling north, we have to go as far as Hammerfest to find proven commercially viable finds. One has also to exercise great care in exploration activities in order not to disturb the spawning of the vital cod stocks around Lofoten/Vesterålen. Northwest of Hammerfest (roughly 120 km) lies the Snøhvit oilfield, together with Albatross and Askeladden with recoverable gas. These will be transported to Melkøya north of Hammerfest harbour for treatment and export by ship. No commercially viable finds have yet been made between Hammerfest and the demarcation line with Russia in the Barents Sea, but the editor is optimistic for the future of the Barents Sea as the Russians have found deposits on their side of the line.

West of and running parallel to the Coastal Express' course a pipeline system lies on the seabed. Oil and gas is transported south to Europe through the complex system. The system starts well north of Norne (west of Sandnessjøen) via Åsgard. Oil from several fields is pumped in along its route and is carried to Kårstø (860 km). Another pipeline (245 km.) runs from Åsgard to the methane production plant at Tjeldbergodden. A new pipeline will also be laid from Haltenbanken along the bottom of the Trondheimsfjord to Skogn near Levanger where our first gas-driven power station will be built. Our politicians make the decision as to whether our gas can be used to generate electric power. It's to be hoped that technology can dispel fears of pollution.

From the Statfjord field, (west of Florø) oil and gas is collected in a giant pipeline system that leads to both the coast if Norway and directly to other European destinations. We have ten pipelines to foreign destinations: Three to Emden in Germany, one to Zeebrugge in Belgium, one to Dunkerque in France, one to Teeside in England, three to St. Fergus in Scotland and one to the Shetlands.

The Coastal Express is the world's most beautiful voyage. But it also sails past a financial fairy-tale country, with oil and gas production worth 200 billion Norwegian kroner annually. This won't last for ever, but fish resources in the fairways sailed by the Coastal Express bring in between 25 -30 billions annually – and best of all, this is a sustainable resource that can be developed and expanded in the future. Norway needs the sea, just as she always has done.

N

W · E

S

Svinøy Fyr

Valderøya
Giske Ålesund lufthavn
Godøy
Langevåg **Ålesund**
Sula Spjelkavik
Runde

Brattvåg
Søvik Vatne

Fosnavåg
Herøy **Torvik**
Hareid Hjørungavåg
Ulsteinvik
Dolsteinsholm
Gurskøy
Vestkapp
Ervik
Stadlandet
Stadhavet
Ånnylysfjorden

Stordfjorden
Sykkylven

Vartdalsfjorden

Ørsta
Volda

Kråkenes Fyr
Einevarden
Klovningen
Veststeinen
Måløy
Vågsøy
Raudeberg
Skongenes Fyr
Selje
Kloster

Nordfjord

Nordfjordeid

Bremanger
Frøya
Kalvåg
Svelgen
Botnane
Frøysjøen

Hornelen
Vingen

Ålfotbreen

Hjelmeset
Sandane

Strym
Lo
Old

Hovden
Batalden
Stabben Fyr
Ytterøyane Fyr
Skorpa
Kinn

Florø
Florø Lufthavn

Jostedalsbreen

Snorre

Murchinson

Askrova
Svanøy
Stavenes
Førdefjorden

Naustdal
Jølster

Førde

Jølster

Statfjord

Alden
Atløy
Askvoll
Dale
Korssund
Vilnesfjorden

Førde Lufthavn

Fjærland

Gullfaks

Ospa
Gåsvær
Utvær Fyr
Sula
Solund Kirke
Steinsund
Ytre Sula

Hyllestad
Lavik
Vadheim
Høyanger

Balestrand
Herman
Leikanger

Sognefjorden

Viksøyri

Veslefrikk

Sogneoksen
Holmengrå Fyr
Gulafjorden

Eivindvik

Stølsheimen

Fedje
Hellisøy Fyr
Fensfjorden
Vardøtangen
Mongstad

Gudvangen

Troll

Oseberg

Hellesøy
Radøy
Sture
Herdla
Holsnøy
Manger
Alver
Knarvik
Kollsnes
Sellashus
Ågotnes
Toftøy
Fana

Dale
Stanghelle

Myr
Voss

Brage

Ytre Arna
Vaksdal
Indre Arna

Ulvik

Straume
Askøy
Bergen
Bergen Lufthavn
Hetland
Sotra
Vaksdal

Øystese
Norheimsund
Hardangerfjorden

Ålvik
Eidfjord

Lofthus

Klokkarvik
Osøyri

Hardanger

Hårteigen
*
1690

Tyssedal
Odda

Folgefonna
Eitro
Hardangervidda

This is our last day on the Coastal Express for now. The captain refuses to give the order to sail at 'half speed' so that we can stay on board for the whole day. He is eager to berth in Bergen so that the ship can be cleaned and made ready for new passengers before they come on board.

It might be an idea to get up early today, but not before we depart from Måløy. We are already familiar with the place from our morning visit on the journey north. Read about Måløy under Day 2.

We are nearing the end of our journey.
(Photo: Ola Røe)

Nord Fjord. Those of you who do get up to say goodbye to Måløy Island, will have the opportunity to admire the graceful passage of the ship as it glides across Nord Fjord. The fjord widens to the east and forges 90 km inland to Loen and Olden and other tourist attractions in the Vestland Fjords. The rugged coastal areas are a striking contrast to the inner fjord areas where the wind is less fierce and there is less rain. Fertile fruit gardens and the fingers of glaciers stretch out towards glistening lakes and gushing rapids. Both types of landscape have their own distinctive charm and tourists are well advised to experience both.

Next we see Hornelen Mountain to the west and Vingen, the site of a large number of rock carvings, to the east. Read about them under Day 2.

To the south, Frøysjøen opens up to the sea. To the west is Bremanger with the fishing village of Kalvåg beyond it. In Gulen Fjord to the east is the industrial area of Svelgen, located here due to the availability of cheap electricity. Bremanger Smelteverk [Bremanger Smelting Works] has Europe's largest electrical smelting furnace for ferrosilicon.

The magnificent Stabben lighthouse guides ships safely into Florø harbour. (Photo: Billedbyrået)

A little further south is a small arm of the fjord. At Botnane there are groups of burial mounds which date back to the Bronze Age. Further to the east, Ålfotbreen glacier has spread its white mantle over the mountains (1,632 m above sea level). We are now approaching Florø, on the tip of mainland Norway. The islands exert a calming influence on the waves of the Norwegian Sea. The island Batalden has long been a sailing mark - from Vikings on their return journeys from England to torpedo boats on missions from the Shetlands during the war. Stabben lighthouse guides ships to the quay in Florø.

FLORØ

Florø has 11,000 inhabitants, of which half live in the town itself. The municipality is called Flora. Almost 9,000 people subscribe to the two local newspapers. The airport handles over 100,000 passengers every year. Founded in 1860, the town is relatively young. Herring formed the basis for the development of the town. Throughout the entire journey, we have noticed that herring stocks along the coast have fluctuated drastically over the years. Florø is mainly involved in fish farming and producing food for the fish farming industry. Salmon, herring and mackerel are caught for sale on the world market. Florø is the supply base for Statfjord where huge quantities of oil are extracted off the coast to the west (the oil is transported to Mongstad). Shipbuilding is a traditional industry, but the economy has fluctuated greatly. **Kystmuseet** [the Coastal Museum] is a new attraction - exhibits include boats and artifacts from coastal communities along with art exhibitions during the summer. Two of the boats are 'M/S Atløy' and 'Galeasen Svanhild'.

Most of Norway's population has always lived near the coast. Florø has spread as far as is possible. (Photo: Tourist Photo, Willy Haraldsen)

Every year a historical play, 'Kinnaspelet', is staged on **Kinn** Island to the west. The basis for this play is the legend of the Irish princess, Sunniva, who escaped by boat from her heathen suitor and drifted along in the Gulf Stream from Ireland. Sunniva herself landed on Selje (described under Day 2), but her companions ran aground at Kinn. The stone church dates from the 1100s and is reminiscent of Norway's oldest churches in Mosterhamn and on Selje. After departure from Florø, you may catch a glimpse of the island and the strange crevice in the mountain, Kinneklova, directly to the west. Ytterøyane lighthouse flashes off the coast.

Svanøy, an island to the east of the route, is 'the pearl of Sunn Fjord'. In the 16th century, a noble family owned 40% of all the land in Sunnfjord. The land here is fertile and heavily forested. A large stone cross with runic inscriptions was apparently erected by St Olav.

Alden. There are spectacular rock carvings at Stavenes, south of Svanøy Island. Next we head southwest for the island of Alden (481 m above sea level), often referred to as 'the Norwegian Horse', 'the Norwegian Lion' and 'the Blue Man' by fishermen.

The Norwegian coast has many landmarks for seafarers,
one of these being Alden.
(Photo: Billedbyrået)

Ospa is an uninhabited island south-southwest of Geita lighthouse. During World War II, this area saw a great deal of illegal activity, involving 'fishing boats' from the Shetlands, allied agents and weapons. The Germans retaliated by taking hostages and warships (torpedo boats) were used against German shipping. One such torpedo boat was taken near Ospa in 1943. Seven prisoners of war in full uniform are shot by direct order of Hitler to Generaloberst von Falkenhorst. He was convicted as a war criminal after the war.

Glancing at the map in passing, the island group of Sula looks to be impenetrable. Nevertheless, the captain will find a way through Steinsundet Strait. (Photo: Billedbyrået)

Steinsundet. The captain never fails to guide the ship safely through the island group of Solund/Sula, just outside the mouth of Sogne Fjord. See the chart on page 129. Solund municipality comprises 1,700 islands and has 900 inhabitants. As you enter Sognesjøen, it is 200 km to the innermost arm of the magnificent Sogne Fjord. Its greatest depth is 1,308 m, but at the entrance of the fjord, the cold water is held back allowing the relatively warm surface water into the fjord. This means that the Gulf Stream also keeps Norway's longest fjord relatively ice-free during the winter.

Eivindvik, on Gulen Fjord's north coast, is the site of the Gulating Courts and several large stone crosses. Boats from up and down the west coast, and from Norwegian dependencies in the Atlantic, sailed into the fjord every year to attend the courts.

Mongstad lies near Fen Fjord, directly to the east of Holmengrå lighthouse. Oil from the Gullfaks, Troll and Statfjord fields is transported to Mongstad's refinery by ship and, once it has been processed, is shipped to the global market. This means that some 1,600 ships dock here every year. 2.5 million tonnes of petroleum, 2.8 million tonnes of diesel, 0.6 million tonnes of jet fuel as well as liquid gas for Statoil's petro-chemical plants and coke for the aluminium industry are processed here annually. You will see Statoil's gas flame from the ship. Mongstad is also the supply base for the Oseberg field, but oil is taken from the field to Sture via a pipeline (see Day 1).

Just west of Mongstad we'll see Vardetangen, mainland Norway's most westerly point at 4° 56'58" east. Do you remember Norway's most easterly point? It was Hornøy Island by Vardø 31° 10'10" east. Norway is wider than we think - almost the equivalent of Amsterdam to Kiev!

Fens Fjord is located in the centre of Norway's oil-rich area. Large oil fields spread out to the west. On land, Mongstad refines natural riches and exports them to the global market.
(Photo: Billedbyrået, Øystein Klakegg)

Fedje. The fishing community of Fedje has 700 inhabitants and 180 bird species. Hellesøy lighthouse marks the main route to Bergen, with Øygarden to the west and Radøy/Holsnøy to the east. South of Hellesøy lighthouse you can see the giant super tankers at Sturevågen. They are taking North Sea oil on board for export.

We sail east of **Herdla** on the northern tip of Askøy Island. The church at Herdla dates from before 1146, but has been burnt down, rebuilt, torn down and rebuilt again. The main farm on this relatively flat island was previously owned by the baglekongen [the bishops' party king], Filippus Arnesson. Håkon Håkonsson gathered his fleet here before his last journey. The English razed this area to the ground in 1665. In 1940-45 the Germans built an airport and fortress, evacuating all the inhabitants.

When we left Bergen on Day 1, we travelled to the *west* of Askøy, passing Hjelte Fjord, the Viking's sea route to countries in the west. The Shetlands = Hjaltland = Hjelte Fjord. Today, we take the route east of Askøy passing Radøy Island (Manger) to the east. **Askøy** is a separate municipality with 20,000 inhabitants linked to Bergen by Askøy Bridge on its southerly tip.

Salhus. To the east we can see Salhus. The name is derived from the old Norse word 'selahus' meaning an obligation to provide travellers with shelter for the night. Today, we can see the new and magnificent Nordhordaland Bridge linking Bergen to the Bergen-Kristiansund coastal road. The floating section of the bridge measures 1,220 m in length, and the elevated section is 180 m high. The magnificent bridges along the route cannot fail to impress you - Norway's many bridges and tunnels have revolutionised travel on land in the coastal areas. But the sea route taken by the Coastal Express remains 'Coastal Highway No. 1'. It brings you even closer to nature, history and the people and its charm is unrivalled.

BERGEN. The Coastal Express docks at 'The town between the 7 mountains'. The writer of this brochure hopes that this small guide book has been of some use to you and we would like to thank you for travelling with us. The captain looks forward to welcoming new travellers on board. The world's most beautiful sea voyage travels the length of a coastline unrivalled in the world.

The 11 Coastal Express vessels hope to see you again. (Photo: Nancy Bundt)

As we sail along the coast you'll realise the importance of fish to Norwegian coastal communities. This might lead you to ask a number of questions: How far from the coast must you travel before you leave Norwegian territorial waters? How close to the coast can foreign trawlers fish? Before we answer these, we would like to explain a few key terms.

1. The base line is the basis of setting boundaries at sea (The UN Marine Law Commission 1982). It runs between the outermost skerries and points on the coast. The longest Norwegian stretch runs between Træna (near the Polar Circle) and Skomvær, outermost in Lofoten.

2. Sea territory is a belt of 4 nautical miles or 7.4 km outside the base line. Here, Norwegian sovereignty is exercised, but «innocent passage» is allowed. Most coastal states now have a territorial limit of 12 nautical miles.

3. Economic zone (from December 1976). The outer border is 200 nautical miles or 370.4 km from the base line, but does not cross the median line of neighbouring nations. Within this zone, Norway is entitled to the sea's natural resources and is responsible for protecting the environment and regulating scientific studies. These areas of sea measure approximately 2 million km². This is five times the size of Norway.

4. The median line is regulated by agreements between neighbouring nations. It has been agreed with Sweden, Denmark and Great Britain. However, Russia and Norway disagree over where the line is to be drawn in the Barents Sea to the north. This line is 1,700 km long and the countries agree on 3/4 of it, but disagree on an area closer to the coast. As a temporary solution, a 'grey zone' has been agreed where Russia and Norway share quotas, but regulate their own fishing. The whole of the «Grey Zone» equals around 1/2 of mainland Norway in area. The so-called «Smutthull» (loophole) lies outside the economic zone (200 nautical mile line) 370 km out at sea, but the area is vital as a hatchery and nursery for juvenile fish. The Smutthull Agreement of 1999 put a stop to non-regulated fishing here.

The continental shelf is primarily of interest for the extraction of resources on and under the seabed, i.e. the production of oil and gas (see separate section on oil and gas, page 116). Geologists often define the continental shelf as being the seabed to the point at which the continental slope drops steeply to the ocean floor. In legal terms, however, the continental shelf *also* includes the slope itself and areas further out, as far as the shelf's formations reach. Naturally, this region is of great importance as, in the future, Norway will have the technical expertise to exploit resources at far greater depths than today. At some points, the Norwegian Continental Shelf stretches beyond the 200 nautical mile border. The part of the shelf which is at a depth of 600 m, measures around 1 million km^2 or two and a half times the size of Norway.

Jan Mayen, the island out in the Norwegian Sea, does not yet qualify as an economic zone, but does have a fishing limit of 200 nautical miles which forbids foreign vessels from fishing there unless by prior agreement with Norway. The fishing limit boundaries with Iceland and Greenland are fixed and agreed. Svalbard has a Norwegian fishing protection zone which, at present, does not discriminate against foreign fishing vessels. The arrangement is intended to protect fry. There are therefore rules governing equipment and minimum quotas, and all catches must be reported. There are quotas for Norwegian Arctic Cod. Foreign fishing vessels are not permitted to fish in the economic zone. However, the government has granted some countries a certain amount of control and limited fishing rights, usually in return for a favour from the country in question. Sea angling is permitted in all salt water. This means that foreigners and Norwegians can cast their fishing lines from the Coastal Express and in the sea. However, a fishing permit is required for fresh water fishing, i.e. in rivers and inland lakes.

The Norwegian coastguard. When you see the coastguard ships in Sortland (Day 9) you will understand the scale of their task of protecting Norwegian rights in an area covering 2 million km^2 - five times the size of Norway. Norwegian authorities know that the fishing stocks must be protected to secure the future of the many coastal communities which depend solely on fish. The government is therefore cooperating with other countries, and has entered into extensive international agreements to regulate catches. After severe overfishing in the 1970s and 1980s, stocks of fish in the northerly waters are now growing again. Norwegian waters are the location for several of the best-protected and most valuable fishing stocks in the North Atlantic.

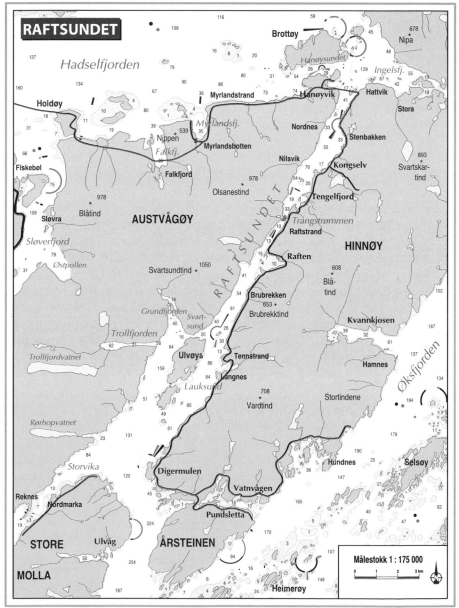

RAFTSUNDET

Kartgrunnlag fra Statens kartverk Sjø • Kartutsnitt ikke tillatt for navigasjon • Tillatelse 412/02

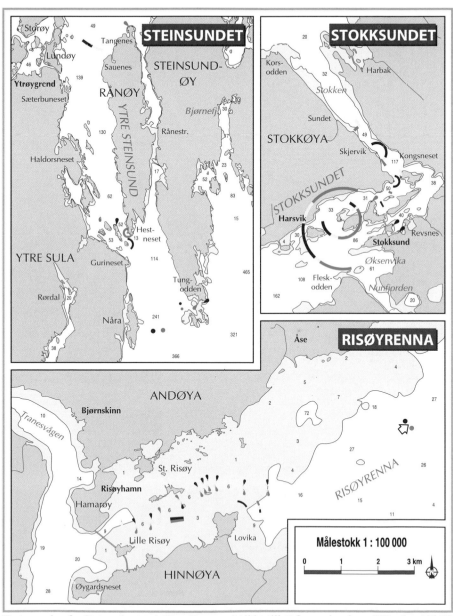

STEINSUNDET

Størøy
Tangenes
Lundøy
Sauenes
STEINSUND-ØY
Ytrøygrend
RÅNØY
Sæterbuneset
YTRE STEINSUND
Bjørnefj.
Rånestr.
Haldorsneset
YTRE SULA
Hest-neset
Gurineset
Rørdal
Nåra
Tung-odden

STOKKSUNDET

Kors-odden
Harbak
Stokken
Sundet
STOKKØYA
Skjervik
Kongsneset
STOKKSUNDET
Harsvik
Revsnes
Stokksund
Øksenvika
Flesk-odden
Nunfjorden

RISØYRENNA

Åse
ANDØYA
Bjørnskinn
Tranesvågen
St. Risøy
Risøyhamn
Hamarøy
RISØYRENNA
Lille Risøy
Lovika
HINNØYA
Øygardsneset

Målestokk 1 : 100 000

0   1   2   3 km

Kartgrunnlag fra Statens kartverk Sjø • Kartutsnitt ikke tillatt for navigasjon • Tillatelse 412/02

KEY TO ROUTE MAP.......

Chart	Town map
Scale 1: 4.000.000	

Chart

Scale 1: 4.000.000

- - - -   Coastal Express route
- - - -   Ferry link
———   Highway
———   Main road
———   Railway

☀ Lighthouse

⛭ Oil and gas field

✈ Small airport

✈ Airport

🐦 Bird colony

🐋 Whale safari

✝ Church

⌘ Atrraction

Town map

🚤 Coastal Express quay

✈ Airport

🚈 Railway

🚌 Bus

ⓘ Tourist Information

✉ Post office

👮 Police

✚ Hospital

⛪ Church

❇ Mountain